MW01006617

"How can we conceiv   a-
tionship with Him? V   th
God and our fellow believers, and when ...   relationships with us? In *Beholding the Invisible, Embracing the Infinite*,
retired attorney Frank Best skillfully deploys abundant and well-
chosen passages of scripture to answer these and other eternal questions and, for good measure, defends the Christian faith against the
assaults of atheists and rival religions. *Beholding the Invisible* is a
must-read for Christians who want to draw closer to God and their
fellow believers and, along the way, equip themselves with informed
responses to those who are critical of our faith."
—Brett Preston, author of One Taken

"Not wild about books about religion? Prepare to be shocked and
delighted. *Beholding the Invisible, Embracing the Infinite* is required
reading for anyone curious about the concepts of faith, eternity and,
well, the meaning of life. Frank Best gives you new and intriguing
takes on the likes of Bertrand Russell, Sigmund Freud, and Erich
Fromm. Does God exist? Is God dead? Will good works get you
where you want to go? You may never think about these questions
the same way after reading this remarkable and accessible volume."
—Royal Oakes, co-host of the podcast Too Many Lawyers

Beholding the Invisible
Embracing the Infinite

Understanding God and
Our Parent/Child Relationship

Franklin L. Best Jr.

RIVER BIRCH PRESS

Daphne, Alabama

ISBN 978-1-956365-29-0 (print)
ISBN 978-1-956365-30-6 (e-book)

For Worldwide Distribution
Printed in the U.S.A.

River Birch Press
P.O. Box 868, Daphne, AL 36526

This book is dedicated to
Dr. James Montgomery Boice
who showed me God from the pulpit of
Tenth Presbyterian Church in Philadelphia

186 - God Father - Ancestum
170 - Legislatura rules
172-73 - Bonhoffer
16 - Father head of house
31 - God as loving Father in OT

Contents

Acknowledgment

My sister, Dana Kuntz, a master of the language, provided immeasurably helpful editing. We do not always agree, especially about commas (see *Eats, Shoots & Leaves* by Lynne Truss, if you are unaware of the comma controversy), so any clumsiness is my fault.

Preface

Even people who are indifferent to God sometimes wonder what the talk of God is all about, such as God bless you, godforsaken, God only knows, and the like. This book will explore what God is like, why God is important to us, and why understanding God is important. It will discuss the God of the Old Testament and the New Testament. It will address the God of the Jews and the Christians, sometimes called Yahweh or Jehovah. It will use the terms "God" and "Lord." As it uses those terms, they will not include Allah, the god of the Koran. It will explain that distinction later.

A person who identifies as neither a Jew nor a Christian may have a purely academic interest in what all the talk is about, but if that is you, beware! You may come away with a relationship you did not anticipate. The Bible (specifically, Paul, in his letter to the Romans) says, "Faith cometh by hearing, and hearing by the word of God" (Romans 10:17).

A person may believe there is a God but may have little sense of who that God is and therefore have little idea of how to relate to that God. Anything that impedes a person's relationship with God is a tragic loss.

The psalms speak eloquently of the richness of a relationship with God. They show us that a relationship with God is two-way: "I love the Lord, because He hath heard my voice and my supplications" (Psalms 116:1). It is the path to wisdom: "The fear of the Lord is the beginning of wisdom" (Psalms 111:10).[1] It provides support: "God is our refuge and strength, a very present help in trouble" (Psalms 46:1). It is a source of joy and celebration: "Sing aloud unto God our strength; make

---

[1] See also Proverbs 9:10, which adds, "The knowledge of the holy is understanding."

a joyful noise unto the God of Jacob . . . Bring hither the timbrel . . . the pleasant harp with the psaltery. Blow up the trumpet" (Psalms 81:1-3). To one who knows Him, God fulfills that person's spiritual needs: "He satisfieth the longing soul, and filleth the hungry soul with goodness" (Psalms 107:9).

David expressed his delight in his relationship with God in the Twenty-Third Psalm, singing, "He maketh me to lie down in green pastures; He leadeth me beside the still waters; He restoreth my soul" (Psalms 23:2-3). David also sang, "In thy presence is fullness of joy" (Psalms 16:11).

The goal of this book is to review what the Bible tells us about understanding God, to provide answers to the merely curious, and to provide insight to those who already know God slightly but could have richer relationships if they had a deeper understanding.

Imagine that a person you did not know said to you, "I am your father." You would want to know more about him to learn more about yourself.

Imagine that he said it warmly. You would begin to explore the possibility of forming a relationship with him.

Imagine that you worked in a business of which he was the founder and Chief Executive Officer. You would want details about him so you could know more about what he expected of you.

Many of us cannot imagine those words without thinking of Darth Vader's saying, "I am your father" to Luke Skywalker in *Star Wars* when Luke accused him of killing Luke's father. If so, imagine reacting completely opposite to Luke's thoughts; despite the bad things some people say about God (some of which will be examined later), this is an entry not into the Dark Side but into the light.

Introduction

God is hard to picture. Thomas Hobbes described the problem: "To attribute figure to Him, is not honor; for all figure is finite: Nor to say we conceive, and imagine, or have an idea of Him, in our mind; for whatsoever we conceive is finite."[2] Not only can we not imagine what God would look like in the event He made Himself visible, but we can hardly imagine what God is like. Thomas Hobbes elaborated: "The nature of God is incomprehensible; that is to say, we understand nothing of *what he is*, but only *that he is*."[3]

God is described as omniscient, omnipotent, omnipresent, and eternal, and none of those seems possible. We can barely imagine such a being, let alone relate to that being. To connect to God, often we attempt to address that problem by ascribing human characteristics to God, resulting in diminishing God. As Michel de Montaigne said, "It is hard to bring matters divine down to human scales without their being trivialized."[4]

Ascribing human characteristics to God can make God subject to ridicule rather than understanding. Richard Dawkins' *The God Delusion* is full of examples, as the title suggests, such as a reference to "[t]he tragi-farce of God's maniacal jealousy against alternative gods."[5]

The Bible, God's communication to humanity, emphasizes that God is other than us. Hosea quotes God as saying, "I am God, and not man" (Hosea 11:9). Numbers says the same thing

---

[2] Thomas Hobbes, *Leviathan,* Oxford World's Classics, 1998, page 240.

[3] *Id.*, page 262.

[4] Michel de Montaigne, *The Complete Essays*, Penguin Books, 1987, page 243.

[5] Richard Dawkins, *The God Delusion*, Mariner Books, 2008, page 279.

and adds an insult to increase the distancing: "God is not a man, that he should lie" (Numbers 23:19). Samuel quotes God as saying to Samuel that God sees "not as man seeth . . . the Lord looketh on the heart" (1 Samuel 16:7). In Psalms 50:21, Asaph quotes God as saying, "Thou thoughtest that I was altogether such an one as thyself: but I will reprove thee."

Some passages emphasize God's grandness in contrast to our insignificance. Isaiah quotes God as saying to us, "My thoughts are not your thoughts, neither are your ways my ways . . . For as the heavens are higher than the earth, so are my ways higher than your ways, and my thoughts than your thoughts" (Isaiah 55:8-9). Peter said, "One day is with the Lord as a thousand years, and a thousand years as one day" (2 Peter 3:8).[6]

God is not only unlike us; there is no other being like God. Isaiah 46:9 says, "I am God, and there is none like me." That follows God's making the same pronouncement five times in Isaiah 45, verses 5, 14, 18, 21, and 22.

God's most personal interaction with a human being was the revelation to Mary that she would bear God's Son, which was through a messenger, the angel Gabriel (see Luke 1:26-38). In the rare instances that men conversed directly with God, God often stayed distant through obscure talk.

When Moses asked God's name, in a direct attempt to understand God, God[7] replied, "I am that I am" (Exodus 3:14).

---

[6] See also Psalms 90:4.

[7] This introduction avoids the use of the pronouns "he," "his," and "him" in referring to God because of their anthropomorphic implications. As the book proceeds, however, it will use those pronouns (with capitalization to show respect) because it makes the writing less stilted, and is consistent with how God has depicted Himself to us. They should be taken as gender-neutral words, which will be explained later.

Later, God gave Moses a long description that nonetheless had a contradiction at its heart: "forgiving iniquity ... and ... visiting the iniquity of the fathers upon the children ... unto the third and to the fourth generation" (Exodus 34:7).

To Job, God was both evasive and emphatic about the gulf between them. Job asked for answers that God did not give. The closest God came to explaining the existence of evil was to say to Job, in effect, "It is what it is." Instead of explaining, God told Job poetically but powerfully that God was vastly unlike Job (and Job was vastly inferior to God). He asked Job, "Where wast thou when I laid the foundations of the earth?" and "Hast thou an arm like God, or canst thou thunder with a voice like him?" (Job 38:4 and 40:9)

Isaiah summarized, "To whom then will ye liken God? Or what likeness will ye compare unto him?" (Isaiah 40:18).

Atheists find the concept of any god absurd. Richard Dawkins, in *The God Delusion*, called God "the great unknown":

> To suggest that the first cause, the great unknown which is responsible for something existing rather than nothing, is a being capable of designing the universe and of talking to a million people simultaneously, is a total abdication of the responsibility to find an explanation.[8]

In *The Closing of the American Mind*, Allan Bloom criticized what he identified as a trend in America to openness to all ideologies and beliefs, with no one having the right to say one opinion is better than the others.

He asked, "Have we so simplified the soul that it is no

[8] Richard Dawkins, *The God Delusion*, Mariner Books, 2008, page 185.

longer difficult to explain?"[9] That leaves two possible understandings of life: accepting that openness so that there is no absolute truth, and therefore no monotheistic god; or rejecting it so that the soul is still challenging to explain. If the soul is difficult to explain, how much more so God?

Despite that strangeness, God has provided an image to make God, and our relationship with God, understandable throughout the Bible. To use the language of Isaiah, God has suggested a likeness to which we can compare God, to have some understanding of God and some guide in knowing how to relate to God. That is the image of God the Father, head of the house of God.

One may respond that there is nothing remarkable about that image, in that the Lord's Prayer is well known, and it begins with "Our Father." In fact, many people call that prayer "the Our Father." And, further, *father* is just another among several metaphors for God, such as the well-known start to the Twenty-Third Psalm, "The Lord is my shepherd," and the familiar hymn, "A Mighty Fortress Is Our God."

Indeed, metaphors for God abound, and *father* in the Lord's Prayer is one of the best known, but that's only a starting point. The image of God the Father, head of the house of God, is far more than the opening to the Lord's Prayer, and it is far more developed than any other metaphor for God. It pervades Scripture in vividness and richness.

Still, as we dive into the extensive scriptural references to the images of God as Father, we must maintain a reverential understanding that they are only metaphors provided to give

---

[9] Allan Bloom, *The Closing of the American Mind*, Simon & Schuster, 1987, page 43.

us an inkling of God, who is vastly more than those scanty metaphors. God tells us in Job that demanding revelation from Him that would enable us to understand Him completely would sacrilegiously inflate us and dishonor God. The image of God as Father tells us much but remains only an outline. As Rene Descartes described its limits:

> [W]e have in the notion of God absolute immensity, simplicity and a unity that embraces all other attributes; and of this idea we find no example in us ... [W]e recognize that none of the particular attributes which we, owing to the limitations of our minds, assign piecemeal to God, ... belong to Him and to us in precisely the same sense.[10]

---

[10] Rene Descartes, Supplementary Passages, *The European Philosophers From Descartes to Nietzsche,* The Modern Library, Random House, 1960, page 84.

Immortal, invisible,
God only wise,
In light inaccessible
hid from our eyes
—*Walter Chalmers Smith*

1

GOD AND GENDER

Before starting to study the house of God, considering the hazards of attempting "to bring matters divine down to human scales," in Montaigne's words, a review of God and gender is in order.

The references throughout the Old and New Testament books to God as Father appear to many people to attribute the male gender to God. The first question in considering the meaning of God's role as Father is to ask whether that attribution of gender to God is appropriate.

God revealed Himself to us through Scripture using human imagery. At the same time, He warned us that our ways are not His ways in Isaiah 55:8. He presumably described Himself using human characteristics because we can understand beings only in a human frame of reference. We need that frame of reference to understand God's nature. Also, some resemblance in some form exists because "God created man in his own image" (Genesis 1:27).

However, any characterization of God in anthropomorphic terms presents a danger of diminishing God and creating confusion. Examples include references to whether God changes His mind.

Before the flood, "It repented the Lord that he had made man on the earth" (Genesis 6:6). However, Balaam told Balak, speaking the words the Lord had put in his mouth, that "God is not a man, that he should lie; neither the son of man, that he should repent" (Numbers 23:19). Each of those passages conveys a truth about God. Yet, put side by side, they appear to contradict each other. The problem lies in describing God in terms of the characteristics of man since "God is not a man."

Attributing gender to God presents a danger of diminishing God and creating confusion. If we think of God as having characteristics of gender, we must understand that He has attributes of both genders.

The implication that God is male, resulting from characterizing God as Father (as well as from choosing the male pronoun for God), is an offense to many. In her search for a feminist philosophy of religion, Grace Jantzen described that characterization as "the Big Daddy in the sky, the One Father God, omnipotent, separate from the universe of which 'he' presides." She rejected that characterization, saying, "In whatever way the divine may be thought, it should not be like that."[1]

No one should be offended or misled by attempts to describe God that connote a specific human gender. God has qualities that traditions have considered feminine as much as those that traditions have considered masculine.

"God is love" (1 John 4:8, 16). Traditions have treated love as a predominantly feminine trait. That is not to say that men do not love. Nonetheless, love has been more strongly associated with women than with men. Women demonstrate love in the physical roles that childbearing women play in nurturing their children. First, a mother carries her child in her womb for nine months. Then she risks death and endures consid-

---

[1] Grace Jantzen, *Becoming Divine*, Indiana University Press, Bloomington, Indiana, 1999, page 7.

erable pain to give birth to the child. She follows those dramatic acts with nursing the child, which represents the essence of nurturing. No matter how loving a father is, nothing that he can do in the routine of daily life can match the power of either the symbolism or the reality of those acts.

God, as the creative Father, made man effortlessly in Eden. However, when God came to live among men as Jesus to die in atonement for our sins so that we may be born again into eternal life, He endured both pain and self-sacrificing death as though it were childbirth. Following that, God provided, and continues to provide, the nurturing associated with a nursing mother through the Holy Spirit, whom He calls the Comforter (John 14:16, 26; 15:26).

The Old Testament describes God as providing comfort of a traditionally feminine quality. Psalms 91 says, "Surely He shall deliver thee from the snare of the fowler, and from the noisome pestilence. He shall cover thee with his feathers, and under his wings shalt thou trust" (Psalms 91:3-4).

David (who did not write Psalms 91) used similar imagery. In Psalms 17:8-9, he asked God to "Keep me as the apple of the eye, hide me under the shadow of thy wings, from the wicked that oppress me, from my deadly enemies, who compass me about" He spoke again of the shelter of God's wings in Psalms 36:7, Psalms 57:1, Psalms 61:4, and Psalms 63:7.

Hymn writers have continued that theme. William Cushing wrote:

Under His wings I am safely abiding; tho' the night deepens and tempests are wild,

Still I can trust Him; I know He will keep me; He has redeemed me, and I am His child.

3

Under His wings, under His wings, who from His love can sever?

Under His wings my soul shall abide, safely abide forever.

In "Jesus, Lover of My Soul," Charles Wesley wrote:

Other refuge have I none, hangs my helpless soul on thee;
Leave, ah! leave me not alone, still support and comfort me!
All my trust on thee is stayed, all my help from thee I bring;
Cover my defenseless head with the shadow of thy wing.

Sheltering chicks under wings is not a behavior associated with male birds. It is behavior that we distinctly associate with female birds.[2] Jesus said so when attributing that characteristic to Himself: "O Jerusalem, Jerusalem . . . how often would I have gathered thy children together, as a hen doth gather her brood under her wings, and ye would not!" (Luke 13:34. See also Matthew 23:37).

Genesis 1:1 tells us that God existed at the beginning, saying, "In the beginning God...." John 1:1 tells us that Jesus existed at the beginning: "In the beginning was the Word, and the Word was with God, and the Word was God." Proverbs 8:22 includes wisdom with both God the Father and God the Son as existing at the beginning. Declaring that wisdom has been "established from everlasting," and that the Lord created the earth by wisdom, when wisdom "was beside Him," reveals that wisdom is a key element of God, and wisdom is presented in a feminine context in the final verses of Proverbs Chapter 9. The seductress calls out, sitting "at the door of her house, on

---

[2] These are associations commonly made according to traditional concepts of masculinity and feminity. In fact, in some species of birds, the male bird shelters with his wings.

a seat by the highest places of the city," to those who pass by, "Whoever is simple, let him turn in here" (Proverbs 9:14-16). Wisdom, likewise, "has built her house," and "from the highest places of the city," cries out, "Whoever is simple, let him turn in here!" (Proverbs 9:3,4) Showing the competition for the simple man between the seductress and wisdom shows the choice men must make between worldly and godly behavior.

When God speaks of the rebellion of the nation of Israel, repeatedly He presents Himself as a husband and Israel as an adulterous wife who played the harlot. The most dramatic example is the Book of Hosea, in which he instructed Hosea to act out that relationship by taking "a wife of whoredoms" (Hosea 1:2). The image is also used throughout the book of Jeremiah and elsewhere in the Old Testament. However, when speaking in Proverbs of the simple rejection of the Lord by individuals, God switches genders. There, the rebel is a man choosing a harlot over wisdom. The instructions to avoid immoral women in Proverbs 5 through 7 are repeated warnings about behavior that is both dangerous to the human being and unfaithful to the Lord.[3]

When God created man in Eden, He created man in His own image, and that image is both male and female. "Then God said, 'Let us make man in our image, after our likeness'. .. So God created man in his own image; in the image of God created he him; male and female created he them" (Genesis 1:26-27). That passage states that God's image, when expressed in human form, is both male and female.

---

[3] References to Wisdom in Proverbs use feminine pronouns, but too much significance should not be assigned to that. Hebrew refers to Wisdom with feminine forms because the grammatical gender of the noun chokmah, "wisdom", is feminine. Using "it" and "its" would also be valid.

God challenged Job with the question, "Who hath divided a watercourse for the overflowing of waters . . . to cause it to rain?" (Job 38:25-26). By opening His speech to Job with the words, "I laid the foundations of the earth" (Job 38:4), God clarified that the answer is that God causes it to rain. So, when God repeats the question, "Hath the rain a father . . . out of whose womb came the ice?" (Job 38:28-29), the answer again is God. The imagery is of both fatherhood and motherhood.

Zephaniah mixes the traditionally female image of singing over the child with the historically masculine image of salvation by the "mighty" Lord (Zephaniah 3:17). Not just that verse, but the whole book of Zephaniah mixes masculine and feminine imagery. Zephaniah's description of God's motherly singing over Jerusalem follows his prophecy of God's fatherly wrath in the day of the Lord. In the context of the Day of the Lord, we think of the voice of the Lord in the way David describes it in the Twenty-Ninth Psalm:

> *The voice of the Lord is upon the waters; the God of glory thundereth; the Lord is upon many waters. The voice of the Lord is powerful; the voice of the Lord is full of majesty. The voice of the Lord breaketh the cedars; yea, the Lord breaketh the cedars of Lebanon . . . The voice of the Lord shaketh the wilderness . . . and in his temple doth everyone speak of his glory* (Psalms 29:3-9).

However, Zephaniah tells us that after the Day of the Lord, God sings to Jerusalem rather than thundering.

Similarly, Isaiah mixes images of might and authority on one hand with gentleness and support on the other:

> *Behold, the Lord God will come with strong hand, and his arm shall rule for him: behold, his reward is with him, and his work before him. He shall feed his flock like a shepherd: he shall gather the lambs with his arm, and carry them in his bosom, and shall gently lead those that are with young* (Isaiah 40:10-11).

The mixed images of both genders vividly depict God's blending of traditionally masculine and feminine characteristics.

At the same time, "God is not a man," Numbers 23:19, which is to say, God is not a human being. In God's true form, God is neither truly male nor truly female. God carries that absence of gender through in relating to His children. God favors neither gender. When God considers His children, He says, "There is neither male nor female; for ye are all one in Christ Jesus" (Galatians 3:28).

Part of the problem with the standard view of the masculinity of God, formed in ignorance of God's traits as described in the Bible, is that the masculine characteristics ascribed to God are exaggerations that do a disservice not only to God but also to all men. Those distorted views of masculinity make sharing traditionally feminine traits seem impossible. For example, Robert Bellah, in *The Broken Covenant*, contrasts Christianity and Judaism with new religions as follows:

> [W]hereas biblical religions are oriented to a sky god, the new religions, explicitly or implicitly, seem more oriented to an earth goddess: Unlike the religions of the sky father this tradition celebrates Nature as mother. The sky religions emphasize the paternal, hierarchical, legalistic and ascetic, whereas the earth tradition emphasizes the maternal, communal, expressive and joyful aspects of existence.[4]

There is indeed hierarchy even within the Godhead, with God the Father and God the Son, which is conducted further with Jesus as the firstborn among the children of God. But

---

[4] Robert Bellah, *The Broken Covenant*, The Seabury Press, 1975, pages 159-160.

otherwise, within the children of God, no hierarchy exists. This book will show that the paternal aspects are often more parental than paternal and have maternal as well as paternal qualities. It will disprove the legalistic and ascetic allegations. It will also show that God has qualities Mr. Bellah described as maternal: the image of the extended family is communal, and God's expressive and joyful aspects will be seen repeatedly.

We should avoid attributing gender to God when thinking of God as Father. Attributing gender to God reduces God to something finite and incomplete. The word *father* is gender-specific, as is the pronoun *he*, and the constant use of those words tempts us to see God as "the Big Daddy in the sky."

We can nonetheless avoid limiting God to a masculine personality, despite those gender-specific words, by remembering that the essential characteristic of a father that describes God is not the father's gender. The important characteristic of fatherhood is the father's parental relationship with his children.

In relating to His children, God does behave in ways that, among humans, are traditionally characteristic of males, and it is helpful to recognize the similarities. However, we can avoid limiting God to maleness by remembering the ways He relates to His children that are traditionally characteristic of females among humans (and others among His creatures).

2

THE TERM *HOUSE*

The extensive references throughout the Bible to God as Father do not stand alone. They are supported by the image of God's children relating to God, to each other, in a family enterprise identified as the house of God. Understanding God as Father involves understanding the house of God. Understanding both enriches our relationship with God, answers many questions about God, and responds to many objections to God, as will be examined later.

According to the King James Version of the Bible, Jesus said that in His Father's house are many mansions (John 14:2). The Greek word translated "mansions" is μονα. It also translated as "dwelling-place," "abode," or simply "room." Some versions, including the Revised Standard Version and the New International Version, say, "In my Father's house are many rooms."

However, the King James translators had good reason to feel comfortable with something grander than mere rooms. The word *house* usually means a building used as a residence, but it can have broader meanings.

Consider, for example, in Edgar Allen Poe's *The Fall of the House of Usher*, the term "House of Usher," which was "an appellation which seemed to include, in the minds of the peasantry who used it, both the family and the family mansion."[5]

Poe played with the ambiguity of the word *house*, to refer to the family and the mansion. Jesus may have similarly played with the meanings of that word. If so, there was a special meaning in Jesus' response to Peter's asking where He was going by referring to His Father's house. That would have invited the listeners to think of a house as a structure, an object to go to. Jesus would then have surprised them by referring to mansions in the house, making them reconsider the meaning of *house*.

Our reverence for Jesus may lead us to imagine His use of language to be austere, but that would color Jesus too blandly. Jesus elsewhere showed His interest in playing with words. He played with the similarities and differences in the Greek words πετρος, meaning "stone," and πετρα, meaning "rock." He said to Simon, "Thou art Peter [πετρος], and upon this rock [πετρα] I will build my church" (Matthew 16:18). He may have been doing similar wordplay with *house*.

The Greek word translated "house" in John 14:2, οικια, can mean a building used as a residence, and that kind of house could not have mansions within it. However, οικια can also mean a household. So can the other Greek word commonly used for house in the New Testament, οικος. A house, therefore, is not necessarily a structure that could only contain rooms. It could be an extended family, which could occupy many mansions. Of course, the word *mansions* is a mere metaphor for a magnificent place to be, but we should not back away from that term out of concern that God's house could not accommodate large numbers of them.

---

[5] Edgar Allan Poe, *The Portable Poe*, Penguin Books 1977 edition, pages 246-247.

Thinking of God's house as an extended family not only helps us understand how it could contain many mansions. It also helps us understand better our relationship with God. That description of our relationship to God occurs throughout the Old and New Testaments in references to houses in general, God's house specifically, fathers as heads of houses, God as Father, believers as children of God, and God's inheritance for His children.

3

OLD TESTAMENT
HEAD OF THE HOUSE

The Old Testament is replete with references to houses, both as family residences and as families themselves, and mentions the house of God as a place to worship God and as those who know God. It also points to the father as the head of the house and refers to God as Father, the head of the house of God.

HOUSES

The Hebrew word translated as "house" has dual meanings of the family and the family residence that Poe tinkered with in *The Fall of the House of Usher*. It has more nuances as well.

The Old Testament often uses it to refer to a residential structure. For example, at Passover, the children of God put blood on "the two side posts and on the upper door post of the houses" (Exodus 12:7). Zimri "burnt the king's house over him" (1 Kings 16:18). The Shulamite woman sang to her beloved that "the beams of our house are cedar and our rafters of fir" (Song of Solomon 1:17). The Lord warned, "Ye have built houses of hewn stone, but ye shall not dwell in them" (Amos 5:11).

The Lord said He will send a curse into the thief's house

and the house of the one who swears falsely by his name. He said, "It shall remain in the midst of his house, and shall consume it with the timber thereof and the stones thereof" (Zechariah 5:4). That passage suggests imagery and a broader meaning, despite the references to timber and stones.

The word *house* also means the family headed by a patriarch. Terah's house consisted of his son Abram; Abram's wife, Sarai; and Terah's grandson Lot (Genesis 11:31-12:1). Zabdi's house included his grandson Achan, who had his own children (Joshua 7:17-24). The members of Terah's house and the members of Zabdi's house included children, grandchildren, and great-grandchildren, as well as their wives.

House means not only a family at a point in time but also a family of descendants extending through many generations. The phrases "house of Israel" and "house of David" are used that way throughout the Old Testament. One example is the Lord's telling David, through Nathan, that "the sword shall never depart from thine house" because David killed Uriah the Hittite and took his wife (2 Samuel 12:10). Another is Jonathan's making a covenant between his house and David's house (1 Samuel 20:15-16). Jonathan expressly said that he was referring to his descendants and David's descendants (1 Samuel 20:42).

It has a fourth meaning that is an extension of the second. It combines the patriarch's extended family with his estate, which is all of his land, buildings, and other possessions. His estate includes his economic enterprise, which is, in effect, a family business.

When four kings took Lot captive, Abraham went after Lot with "his trained servants, born in his own house, three hundred and eighteen" (Genesis 14:14). Three hundred eighteen people were not born in a residence, particularly considering that Abraham lived in a tent (see Genesis 18:1). Instead, they were born in the business enterprise that Abraham headed. Abraham circumcised not only Ishmael but also "every male among the men of Abraham's house" (Genesis 17:23).

When Simeon and Levi took vengeance on Hamor and Shechem, they "came upon the city, boldly, and slew all the males." They "spoiled the city, because they had defiled their sister. They took their sheep, and their oxen, and their asses, and that which was in the city, and that which was in the field, and all their wealth . . . and spoiled even all that was in the house" (Genesis 34:25-29). Jacob complained to Simeon and Levi, "Ye have troubled me to make me stink among the inhabitants of the land . . . and I shall be destroyed, I and my house" (Genesis 34:30).

In the case of a king, *house* can refer not only to the king's extended family and servants but also to all loyal to the king. After Ahab was killed in battle at Ramoth Gilead, the Lord anointed Jehu king of Israel and directed him to "smite the house of Ahab," to the extent that "the whole house of Ahab shall perish" (2 Kings 9:7-8). Jehu did "unto the house of Ahab according to all that was in [the Lord's] heart" (2 Kings 10:30. To do that, he killed: Ahab's wife Jezebel (2 Kings 9:33); Ahab's son Jehoram, who was the king of Israel (2 Kings 9:24); Ahaziah, king of Judah, who was described in 2 Kings 8:27 as "the son in law of the house of Ahab" (2 Kings 9:27), as well as "the sons of the brethren of Ahaziah, that ministered to Ahaziah" (2 Chronicles 22:8); all seventy of Ahab's sons in Samaria (2 Kings 10:7); all of Ahab's "great men, and his kinsfolks, and his priests" (2 Kings 10:11); "all that remained unto Ahab in Samaria" (2 Kings 10:17); and all of the worshipers of Ahab's god, Baal (2 Kings 10:21-28).

Habakkuk used dual imagery in one statement: "Thou hast consulted shame to thy house by cutting off many people . . . for the stone shall cry out of the wall, and the beam out of the timber shall answer it" (Habakkuk 2:10-11).

HOUSE OF THE LORD

Many references to the house of the Lord refer to a structure. In the time of the judges, the house of God was in Shiloh (Judges 18:31; 1 Samuel 1:24). The people of Israel "went up to the house of God, and asked counsel of God" (Judges 20:18). They also "came unto the house of God, and wept," and "sat there before the Lord, and fasted . . . and offered burnt offerings and peace offerings before the Lord" (Judges 20:26). When David's first son by Bathsheba died, David "came into the house of the Lord, and worshiped" (2 Samuel 12:20). In those days, the house of the Lord was a tent (2 Samuel 7:6).

When another son of Bathsheba, Solomon, became king, he built the temple in Jerusalem to be the house of the Lord (1 Kings 6:1–8:66). Subsequently, Ahaz "shut up the doors of the house of the Lord" (2 Chronicles 28:24). After Ahaz died, his son, Hezekiah, "opened the doors of the house of the Lord, and repaired them" (2 Chronicles 29:3).

However, other references to the house of the Lord do not refer to a structure. When David sang that he would dwell in the house of the Lord all his days, he did not mean the place of worship where he mourned his son (Psalms 23:6). When the Lord told Aaron and Miriam that Moses was "faithful in all mine house" (Numbers 12:7), He was not speaking of a building.

David spoke of God's house in the non-structural sense when he said, "The children of men put their trust under the shadow of thy wings," and "shall be abundantly satisfied with the fatness of thy house" (Psalms 36:7-8). He spoke there of the provision and protection enjoyed by the household members.

The implications of using the term *house*, combined with the contexts of the references to the house of God, are extensive. Not only is the house of God, in its broadest sense, not merely a structure, but it also extends to include many people and to continue in time. That is shown by citing God as the head of the household and describing members of the household and their relationships to God and each other.

THE FATHER, AS HEAD OF THE HOUSE

The master of the house was the father. The house is identified as the house of the father. The Lord told Abram to "Get thee out . . . from thy father's house" (Genesis 12:1). The father determined the relationship with God for the house. Joshua declared that "as for me and my house, we will serve the Lord" (Joshua 24:15).

The father instructed his children. The proverbs are presented as instruction from a father to his children. See Proverbs 1:8; 2:1; 3:1; 4:1, 10; 5:1; 6:20; 7:1, 24; 8:32; 13:1; 15:5; 23:15, 19, 22. The father followed up on instruction with enforcement, which is a principle that is described in Proverbs 13:24: "He that spareth his rod hateth his son: but he who loveth him chasteneth him betimes." It is repeated in other Proverbs:

Chasten thy son while there is hope (Proverbs 19:18).

Withhold not correction from the child: for if thou beatest him with the rod, he shall not die. Thou shalt beat him with the rod, and shalt deliver his soul from hell (Proverbs 23:13-14).

The rod and reproof give wisdom but a child left to himself bringeth his mother to shame . . . Correct thy son, and he shall give thee rest; yea, he shall give delight unto thy soul (Proverbs 29:15, 17).

The head of the house oversaw protecting the members of the house. A family member other than the father could save the family, as in the case of Rahab's saving her father's household (Joshua 2:12-19; 6:22-25). Nonetheless, protecting the household members was the father's responsibility, and if any member became lost, the father was to retrieve him. Abraham rescued Lot when he was carried away from Sodom in an attack by four kings (Genesis 14:1-16). David rescued his wives, and the wives and children of his men, when the Amalekites carried them away from Ziklag (1 Samuel 30:1-18). Job took measures to save his sons spiritually. He regularly rose early in the morning to offer burnt offerings for his sons, reasoning, "It may be that my sons have sinned, and cursed God in their hearts" (Job 1:5).

The head of the house was the spiritual leader of the home. Proverbs 4:10-11 says, "My son . . . I have led thee in right paths" (Proverbs 4:10-11). The father set an example by saying, "I will walk within my house with a perfect heart" (Psalms 101:2). He avoided bad models for the household by laying down the rule, "He that worketh deceit shall not dwell within my house" (Psalms 101:7).

The father's spiritual strength benefited the entire family. The Lord invited into the ark not just Noah but all his family as well (Genesis 7:1). Along with Noah, Noah's wife, his sons, and his sons' wives entered the ark (Genesis 7:13). Noah's house was saved because Noah was righteous and because Noah found grace in the eyes of the Lord (Genesis 6:8, 7:1).

17

On the other hand, the father's drunken nakedness polluted the family for generations. Noah cursed Canaan, a son of Ham, for Ham's seeing his nakedness (Genesis 9:20-27). In the Ten Commandments, God warned about "visiting the iniquity of the fathers upon the children unto the third and fourth generation of them that hate me" (Exodus 20:5). Again, in proclaiming His name to Moses, He declared, "The Lord God . . . visiting the iniquity of the fathers upon the children, and upon the children's children, unto the third and to the fourth generation" (Exodus 34:6-7).

The continuation of a house was achieved through inheritance from the father. A man could build a large business enterprise with many workers and their families and, in that sense, have a great house. However, it would be only a short-term house if it did not live on after him. He needed children, to continue both the family line and the family enterprise through inheritance. The results of his efforts in building his house would be short-lived if he did not have a son to inherit it. Abram wanted a son not just because of parental urges but because, as he told the Lord, without a son, his heir would be his servant, Eliezer of Damascus (Genesis 15:2).

GOD THE FATHER AS HEAD OF THE HOUSE OF GOD

The Old Testament does not merely tell of the house of God; it expressly calls God the Father of believers. It calls God Father throughout the law, the writings, and the prophets.

The Lord told the Jews through Moses, "Ye are the children of the Lord your God" (Deuteronomy 14:1). David said, "Blessed be thou, Lord God of Israel our father, for ever and ever" (1 Chronicles 29:10). David called God "a father of the fatherless" (Psalms 68:5). Isaiah said to the Lord, "Thou art our father" (Isaiah 63:16; 64:8).

Some of the references are about Israel as the child of God. Through Jeremiah, the Lord said, "I am a father to Israel" (Jeremiah 31:9). The Lord told Moses to tell Pharaoh, "Israel is my son, even my firstborn" (Exodus 4:22). Scripture described that relationship as involving initial closeness followed by Israel's rebellion, with the Lord's sparing Israel, followed by reconciliation.

Hosea quotes the Lord's tenderly describing the early stage of his fatherly relationship with Israel: "When Israel was a child, then I loved him, and called my son out of Egypt . . . I taught Ephraim also to go, taking them by their arms . . . I drew them . . . with bands of love . . ." (Hosea 11:1-4).

Deuteronomy quotes Moses similarly describing God's early relationship with Israel: "He shall fight for you, according to all that he did for you in Egypt before your eyes; and in the wilderness, where thou hast seen how that the Lord thy God bare thee, as a man doth bear his son . . ." (Deuteronomy 1:30-31).

After that youthful period, however, Israel rebelled. Immediately after telling how God carried Israel as a father holds his son, Moses said, "Yet . . . ye did not believe the Lord your God" (Deuteronomy 1:32). The Lord told Isaiah, "I have nourished and brought up children, and they have rebelled against me" (Isaiah 1:2). The Lord told Ezekiel He was sending him to prophesy to Israel because "they are impudent children and stiffhearted" (Ezekiel 2:4). The Lord said to Israel, through Jeremiah, "Wilt thou not from this time cry unto me, My father, thou art the guide of my youth?" (Jeremiah 3:4)

The Lord reacted as a father turning away from his family.

He said, "Where is the bill of your mother's divorcement, whom I have put away? . Behold ... for your transgressions is your mother put away" (Isaiah 50:1). Moses said, "He abhorred them, because of the provoking of his sons, and of his daughters" (Deuteronomy 32:19). Isaiah reprimanded the children of God for their bad behavior, reporting the Lord's reproof: "Woe to the rebellious children, saith the Lord, that take counsel, but not of me ... Now go, write it before them in a table ... that this is a rebellious people, lying children, children that will not hear the law of the Lord ..." (Isaiah 30:1; 8-9).

Expressing Israel's betrayal requires more than describing Israel as a rebellious child; it also requires the metaphor of an unfaithful wife. That metaphor is most vividly expressed in Hosea. The Lord instructed Hosea to "take unto thee a wife of whoredoms" to demonstrate God's relationship with Israel (Hosea 1:2). The images of playing the harlot, committing adultery, and marital desertion are also used elsewhere throughout the Old Testament, including Leviticus 17:7; Numbers 15:39; 25:1-3; Deuteronomy 31:16; Judges 2:17; 8:27, 33; Isaiah 1:21; Jeremiah 2:20; 3:1, 6, 8-9, 20; 5:7-8; 9:2; 11:15; 13:27; 22:20-22; 23:10, 14; 31:32; Ezekiel 6:9; 16:15-43; 20:30; 23:1-49; 43:7-9; and Micah 1:7.

The metaphor of the adulterous wife intensifies, rather than contradicts, the image of the rebellious child, and the two are sometimes mixed. Hosea's theme of adultery is bracketed by references in chapters 1 and 11 to the children of Israel as sons of God. Jeremiah mixes the metaphors in a single sentence: "Turn, O backsliding children, saith the Lord; for I am married unto you" (Jeremiah 3:14).

Despite the betrayal, the Lord's love for His children remains. Jeremiah quotes the Lord's saying, "Is Ephraim my dear son? Is he a pleasant child? For since I spake against him, I do earnestly remember him still; therefore, my bowels are troubled for him; I will surely have mercy upon him" (Jeremiah 31:20).

Eventually, God will bring Israel back into His family. Isaiah quotes the Lord's promise of reconciliation with His adulterous bride: "In a little wrath I hid my face from thee for a moment; but with everlasting kindness will I have mercy on thee, saith the Lord thy Redeemer" (Isaiah 54:8).

Hosea relays the same message:

> *Therefore, behold, I will allure her, and bring her into the wilderness, and speak comfortably unto her . . . she shall sing there, as in the days of her youth, as in the day when she came up out of the land of Egypt. And it shall be at that day, saith the Lord, that thou shalt call me Ishi [my husband] . . . And I will betroth thee unto me for ever* (Hosea 2:14-19).

Hosea also expresses the reconciliation in terms of the return of rebellious children. Hosea prophesies that after His children backslide, the Lord will bring them back: "They shall walk after the Lord . . . and I will place them in their houses . . ." (Hosea 11:10-11).

The Lord promised, through Jeremiah: "Thou shalt call me, My father; and shalt not turn away from me" (Jeremiah 3:19).

In addition to the father-son relationship between God and Israel, the Old Testament consistently describes God as the Father of individual believers. Those references show God's acting as Father in a variety of ways.

God is our Creator. He is the Father who gave us life. Isaiah said, "But now, O Lord, thou art our father; we are the clay, and thou our potter" (Isaiah 64:8). Malachi said, "Have we not all one father? Hath not one God created us?" (Malachi 2:10).

God did not give us life and walk away from us, as the deists of the Enlightenment believed. As our father, He cares for us. In the first four verses of the Hosea 11, quoted above, God teaches His children to walk and stoops to feed them.

God has compassion for us. David sang, "Like as a father pitieth his children, so the Lord pitieth them that fear him. For he knoweth our frame; he remembereth that we are dust" (Psalms 103:13-14).

God provides to us all that we have. David said, when the contributions were made for the building of the temple, "Blessed be thou, Lord God of Israel our father, for ever and ever . . . for all things come of thee, and of thine own have we given thee" (1 Chronicles 29:10, 14).

God meets not only our physical needs but also our spiritual needs. As a longsuffering Father, God persistently corrects His children. Proverbs explained, "Whom the Lord loveth he correcteth; even as a father the son in whom he delighteth (Proverbs 3:12). Deuteronomy 8:5 says, "Thou shalt also consider in thine heart, that, as a man chasteneth his son, so the Lord thy God chasteneth thee."

As our Father, He is our Redeemer, who retrieved us when we were lost. Moses said, "Is not he thy father that hath bought thee?" (Deuteronomy 32:6). Isaiah said, "Thou, O Lord, art our father, our redeemer" (Isaiah 63:16).

Isaiah described God as redeeming Israel corporately and believers individually: "O Israel, Fear not: for I have redeemed thee . . . I will say to the north, Give up; and to the south, Keep not back: bring my sons from far, and my daughters from the ends of the earth" (Isaiah 43:1, 6).

In His role as Father, because of all He has done for us and who He is, He is worthy of honor and reverence. The Lord said to Israel through Malachi, "If then I be a father, where is mine honour? and if I be a master, where is my fear?" (Malachi 1:6)

4

OLD TESTAMENT MEMBERS

CHILDREN OF GOD

The children of Israel, which is to say the descendants of Jacob, were by birth the children of God. Moses told them, "Ye are the children of the Lord your God . . . For thou art an holy people unto the Lord thy God, and the Lord hath chosen thee to be a peculiar people unto himself" (Deuteronomy 14:1-2). The Lord said to Hosea, "The number of the children of Israel shall be as the sand of the sea . . . And it shall come to pass . . . it shall be said unto them, 'Ye are the sons of the living God'" (Hosea 1:10).

Along with the blessing of that relationship comes responsibility. A child's unruly behavior reflects poorly on the father. Proverbs tells us that a son's sleeping in the harvest or consorting with gluttons causes shame to the father (Proverbs 10:5; 28:7). Similarly, the sins of the children of God reflect badly on God. Nathan told David that his killing Uriah the Hittite and taking his wife, Bathsheba, had "given great occasion to the enemies of the Lord to blaspheme" (2 Samuel 12:14).

THE INHERITANCE

As the father at the head of a household, the Lord passes

on an inheritance to His children. He passes on a physical inheritance and a spiritual inheritance.

Their physical inheritance is the land. The Lord told Abram, "I am the Lord that brought thee out of Ur of the Chaldeans, to give thee this land to inherit it" (Genesis 15:7). Isaac blessed Jacob with the blessing, "God Almighty bless thee ... that thou mayest inherit the land ... which God gave unto Abraham" (Genesis 28:3-4). The Lord told Moses, "I will bring you in unto the land, concerning the which I did swear to give it to Abraham, to Isaac, and to Jacob; and I will give it you for an heritage" (Exodus 6:8). When Joshua took the land, he "gave it for an inheritance unto Israel according to their divisions by their tribes" (Joshua 11:23). Scripture contains many additional references to the land as an inheritance for God's people, including songs about it in Psalms 78, 105, 135, and 136.

Even after Joshua took Canaan, the prophets prophesied a future inheritance of the land. Amos described it as a time of plenty, in which the Lord will provide for His people: "I will plant them upon their land, and they shall no more be pulled up out of their land which I have given them, saith the Lord thy God" (Amos 9:15).

Ezekiel described it as a time not only of a fruitful land but also of protection and closeness with God:

Thus saith the Lord God; When I shall have gathered the house of Israel from the people among whom they are scattered ... then shall they dwell in their land that I have given to my servant Jacob. And they shall dwell safely therein, and shall build houses, and plant vineyards ... they shall know that I am the Lord their God (Ezekiel 28:25-26).

I will bring them out from the people, and gather them from the countries, and will bring them to their own land, and feed them

upon the mountains of Israel by the rivers, and in all the inhab-
ited places of the country . . . I will make with them a covenant
of peace, and will cause the evil beasts to cease out of the land:
and they shall dwell safely in the wilderness, and sleep in the
woods . . . they shall be safe in their land, and shall know that
I am the Lord . . . (Ezekiel 34:13, 25, 27).

I will put my Spirit within you, and cause you to walk in my
statutes, and ye shall keep my judgments, and do them. And ye
shall dwell in the land that I gave to your fathers; and ye shall
be my people, and I will be your God (Ezekiel 36:27-28).

Isaiah's prophesied inheritance clearly transcended possession of a piece of this earth. In the chapter 57, he relays God's
condemnation of the children of Israel as "children of transgression, a seed of falsehood," followed by God's promise that
"he that putteth his trust in me shall possess the land, and shall
inherit my holy mountain" (Isaiah 57:4, 13). The phrase "inherit my holy mountain" could be a poetic repetition, but the
word *holy* suggests a spiritual inheritance.

In the discussion of inheritance that follows, Isaiah begins
with the land:

And I will bring forth a seed out of Jacob, and out of Judah an
inheritor of my mountains: and mine elect shall inherit it, and
my servants shall dwell there. And Sharon shall be a fold of
flocks, and the valley of Achor a place for the herds to lie down
in, for my people that have sought me (Isaiah 65:9-10).

However, that promise of a future inheritance includes
more than earthly mountains and valleys. Isaiah goes on to
prophesy:

For, behold, I create new heavens and a new earth; and the
former shall not be remembered, nor come into mind. But be ye

glad and rejoice for ever in that which I create: for, behold, I create Jerusalem a rejoicing, and her people a joy. And I will rejoice in Jerusalem, and joy in my people: and the voice of weeping shall be no more heard in her, nor the voice of crying (Isaiah 65:17-19).

God promised the land to Abraham in the Abrahamic covenant, but the promise involved much more than the land. God also promised Abraham to make his name great, to multiply his seed, to be God to him and his seed, to bless him and his seed, and to make him and his seed a blessing to others (Genesis 12:1-3, 17:1-8; 26:2-5; 28:13-15).

The blessing extended to the inheritance of everlasting life. The prophecy was given to Daniel that "many of them that sleep in the dust of the earth shall awake, some to everlasting life," and Daniel was told that "thou shall rest, and stand in thy lot [arise to your inheritance] at the end of the days" (Daniel 12:2, 13).

The children of God understood that their inheritance included everlasting life in the kingdom of God and praised God for it. Hannah recited Psalms 113:7 and 8: "The Lord . . . raiseth up the poor out of the dust, and lifteth up the beggar from the dunghill, to set them among princes," and added, "and to make them inherit the throne of glory" (1 Samuel 2:7-8).

WAITING ON THE LORD

Abraham, Isaac, and Jacob had to wait for their descendants to inherit the land. Once Joshua took the land, each child of God had to wait to awake to everlasting life. Although God, as our Father, nurtures us in the present, the promise of the full inheritance lies in the future.

David sang of waiting on the Lord for the inheritance of

the land. He said, "Wait on the Lord, and keep his way, and he shall exalt thee to inherit the land" (Psalms 37:34). By David's time, God had already brought His children into the land He had promised to Abraham, Isaac, and Jacob, so David's song about inheriting the land was a metaphor for spiritual inheritance.

Isaiah said, "I will wait upon the Lord, that hideth his face from the house of Jacob, and I will look for him" (Isaiah 8:17).

Micah connected waiting with salvation, saying, "I will wait for the God of my salvation" (Micah 7:7). Jeremiah spoke directly of waiting for salvation, saying, "The Lord is my portion, saith my soul; therefore will I hope in him . . . It is good that a man should both hope and quietly wait for the salvation of the Lord" (Lamentations 3:24, 26).

Saul was impatient and lost the opportunity to have his house reign over Israel. Samuel told Saul to wait for him in Gilgal. Saul did so for seven days and then made the burnt offering himself rather than leaving that task to Samuel. No sooner had he done that, than Samuel came. Samuel told him, "Thou hast done foolishly . . . for now would the Lord have established thy kingdom upon Israel for ever. But now thy kingdom shall not continue: the Lord hath sought him a man after his own heart" (1 Samuel 13:13-14).

The man that the Lord sought to replace Saul was David. David waited well and established his house to reign over Israel. Saul repeatedly threatened to kill David. Even though David had been anointed to become king, David left the matter to the Lord to deal with in His own way and in His own time. For example, when David and Abishai found Saul asleep with his spear next to him, and Abishai asked David's permission to drive the spear through Saul, David said, "The

Lord shall smite him; or his day shall come to die; or he shall descend into battle, and perish" (1 Samuel 26:10).

Waiting on the Lord can be tiring and frustrating, but to those who do, the Lord gives endurance. Isaiah said:

He giveth power to the faint; and to them that have no might he increaseth strength. Even the youths shall faint and be weary, and the young men shall utterly fall: but they that wait upon the Lord shall renew their strength; they shall mount up with wings as eagles; they shall run, and not be weary; and they shall walk, and not faint (Isaiah 40:29-31).

BROTHERS AND SISTERS

The children of God are brothers and sisters to each other. As brothers and sisters, the children of Israel had special obligations to each other.

Hebrews could take permanent slaves from the nations. Leviticus 25:44-46. In contrast, they were instructed, "If thy brother that dwelleth by thee be waxen poor, and be sold unto thee; thou shalt not compel him to serve as a bondservant: but as an hired servant and a sojourner, he shall be with thee, and shall serve thee unto the year of jubile" (Leviticus 25:39-40). Serving until the year of jubilee meant a fellow Hebrew would serve only for six years, "and in the seventh he shall go out free for nothing" (Exodus 21:2). Not only was the master directed to send him away free, but the law also instructed him: "Thou shalt not let him go away empty: thou shalt furnish him liberally out of thy flock, and out of thy [threshing] floor, and out of thy winepress" (Deuteronomy 15:13-14).

Hebrews were permitted to lend to foreigners at interest (Deuteronomy 23:20). In fact, the Lord promised to the Hebrews that they would lend to many nations (Deuteronomy

15:6; 28:12). However, they were directed, "Thou shall not lend upon usury [charge interest] to thy brother" (Deuteronomy 23:19). Exodus 22:25 also states that prohibition. If a Hebrew took his neighbor's garment as a pledge, he had to return it before nightfall (Exodus 22:26). A Hebrew was permitted to lend to a brother without exacting interest, but after seven years had to release the debt (Deuteronomy 15:1-2). That requirement did not apply to loans to foreigners (Deuteronomy 15:3).

The Hebrews, however, did not follow those instructions. Nehemiah told the nobles and the rulers, "Ye exact usury, every one of his brother" (Nehemiah 5:7). The Lord repeated to Jeremiah His instruction, "At the end of seven years let ye go every man his brother an Hebrew, which hath been sold unto thee; and when he hath served thee six years, thou shalt let him go free from thee," and said, "but your fathers hearkened not unto me, neither inclined their ear" (Jeremiah 34:14).

We are instructed not to criticize our brothers and sisters. Jerusalem condemned Samaria. (That is why Jesus chose a Samaritan for the good Samaritan story; religiously observant Jews could not imagine a good Samaritan). God told Ezekiel to tell Jerusalem:

> *Thou also, which hast judged thy sisters, bear thine own shame for thy sins that thou hast committed more abominable than they: they are more righteous than thou: yea, be thou confounded also, and bear thy shame, in that thou hast justified thy sisters* (Ezekiel 16:52).

We must remember that "He that soweth discord among brethren" is an abomination to the Lord (Proverbs 6:19).

Instead, we should be role models for our brothers and sisters and support them in making the right choices in behavior. When brothers are partners in crime, as were the sons of Eli (1 Samuel 2:12-17) and the sons of Samuel (1 Samuel 8:3), each tragically fails to pull the other up out of his depravity, and instead, they pull each other down.

The Old Testament looks ahead to the Messiah's renewing the brotherly relationship among the children of God by being the chief brother among the brothers and sisters. Psalms 89:27 says, "Also I will make him my firstborn, higher than the kings of the earth."

Many people imagine God in the Old Testament only as judging and punishing. In contrast, the Old Testament depicts God as Father, providing for His household, protecting His children, and tenderly loving them. Contrary to what many believe, the New Testament did not introduce love as an attribute of God. It continued and elaborated on the description of God in the Old Testament.

5

NEW TESTAMENT
HEAD OF THE HOUSE

The Old Testament ends with a family reference in Malachi 4:5 and 6, prophesying that "I will send you Elijah the prophet before the coming of the great and dreadful day of the Lord: and he shall turn the heart of the fathers to the children, and the heart of the children to their fathers."

If the image of God as the head of the extended family, the house of God, in the father's role, ended with Malachi, that image could be dismissed as an obvious characterization of a tribal god. Richard Dawkins called Judaism "originally a tribal cult of a single fiercely unpleasant God, morbidly obsessed with . . . his own superiority over rival gods . . ." [6] Dawkins meant "tribal cult" to be an insult. The Old Testament, however, is unabashed in presenting Yahweh as a tribal god. Only with the coming of the Messiah in the New Testament was a relationship with God made widely available to non-Jews.

When Moses asked God His name, God replied, "Thus shalt thou say to the children of Israel, the LORD [Yahweh] God of your fathers, the God of Abraham, the God of Isaac, and the God of Jacob, hath sent me unto you: this is my name for ever, and this is my memorial unto all generations" (Exodus

---

[6] Richard Dawkins, *The God Delusion*, Mariner Books, 2006, page 58.

3:15). Yahweh's covenant was with Abraham, Isaac, and Jacob (Genesis 28:13; Exodus 2:25). Of course, Yahweh needed to be distinguished from other tribal gods, not to show "superiority over rival gods," as Dawkins scornfully charges, and as would be the natural supposition of any skeptic from Moses' day to the present, but to be clear that Yahweh is the only true God.

What is a tribe but an extended family? Indeed this tribe regarded itself as an extended family, calling itself "the children of Israel." Depicting a tribal god as head of a household may not be surprising. Still, the extensively repeated, descriptively rich use of the image of Yahweh as the Father at the head of the house of God is noteworthy and deeply expressive.

Even more impressive is that image's continuation, along with the images of the children of God and their inheritance, throughout the New Testament. The New Testament also reported expanding the house of God by extensively including non-Jews. One dramatic example is the case of the centurion, as recorded in Matthew 8:5. Later, the apostles, under the direction of the crucified and risen Jesus to "teach all nations" (Matthew 28:19), preached, "Whosoever shall call on the name of the Lord shall be saved" (Acts 2:21). The image of God as Father of the house of God continued, with additions to the family being characterized as rebirths or adoptions. Further, it was vastly enriched by the addition to the family of a Son of God, Jesus, begotten by God the Father.

HOUSES

Much activity in the New Testament took place in residential houses. When word circulated that Jesus was in a house in Capernaum, some people put a hole in the roof through which they lowered a paralytic whom Jesus healed spiritually and physically (Mark 2:1-12). Jesus brought a twelve-year-old girl back to life in the house of her father, Jairus (Mark 5:22-43). When Martha went out to meet Jesus after her brother Lazarus had died, her sister Mary stayed in their house (John 11:20).

On the day of Pentecost, when the Holy Spirit filled the apostles, they were sitting in a house that became filled with a sound from heaven like a mighty rushing wind (Acts 2:2). A possessed man leaped on some itinerant Jewish exorcists in his house and attacked them so violently that they ran out of the house naked (Acts 19:13-16). Priscilla and Aquila had a church in their house (Romans 16:5; 1 Corinthians 16:19).

However, as in the Old Testament, *house* does not mean only a residential structure. The New Testament continues the Old Testament references to the house of Israel and the house of David. For example, Jesus said He was sent, and He sent the twelve, "to the lost sheep of the house of Israel" (Matthew 10:6; 15:24). Luke tells us that Joseph was of the house of David (Luke 1:27; 2:4).

Hebrews describes Jesus as "a son over his own house" (Hebrews 3:6). Jesus said that a house divided against itself will not stand (Matthew 12:25; Mark 3:25). Some people may have an image in their minds' eyes of a building somehow cut down the middle, and Jesus may have intended a double meaning to play on words. Still, just before that, He spoke of a kingdom divided against itself, so the context suggests that Jesus was referring to a household as a group of people.

The rich man in Hades asked Abraham to send someone to his father's house to warn his five brothers (Luke 16:27). He did not ask for someone to knock on his father's door.

Most likely, his father had died before him, especially since he did not ask for a warning to his father as well as to his brothers. Rather than referring to his father's residence, when he spoke of his father's house, he spoke of his father's family.

HOUSE OF GOD

The New Testament sometimes refers to the house of God as a structure. For example, Jesus talked about David's entering the house of God to eat the showbread (Matthew 12:4; Luke 6:4). When Jesus went into the temple and drove out those who bought and sold there, He spoke of the temple when He quoted from Isaiah and Jeremiah, saying, "It is written, My house is the house of prayer: but ye have made it a den of thieves" (Luke 19:46).

However, the New Testament also uses the term to mean something other than a structure. Peter said, "The time is come that judgment must begin at the house of God." He was talking about people, not a building because he said, "If it first begin at us, what shall the end be of them that obey not the gospel of God?" (1 Peter 4:17)

Hebrews quotes 2 Samuel 7:14 as referring to Jesus. The quote in Hebrews is, "I will be to him a Father, and he shall be to me a Son" (Hebrews 1:5). That is part of the instruction the Lord gave Nathan to pass on to David about David's desire to build a temple for the Lord. God said to David:

> *And when thy days be fulfilled, and thou shalt sleep with thy fathers, I will set up thy seed after thee, which shall proceed out of thy bowels, and I will establish his kingdom. He shall build an house for my name, and I will establish the throne of his kingdom for ever. I will be his father, and he shall be my son* (2 Samuel 7:12-14).

To the extent God spoke there concerning Solomon, He used *house* to mean a structure. To the extent that He spoke of Jesus, He used *house* to mean a family. That double usage of *house* is echoed in the New Testament by Paul in Ephesians, also mixing in the metaphor of the commonwealth of Israel:

> *Wherefore remember, that ye being in time past Gentiles in the flesh . . . That at that time ye were without Christ, being aliens from the commonwealth of Israel . . . But now in Christ Jesus . . . Now therefore ye are no more strangers and foreigners, but fellowcitizens with the saints, and of the household of God; and are built upon the foundation of the apostles and prophets, Jesus Christ himself being the chief corner stone; in whom all the building fitly framed together groweth unto an holy temple in the Lord: in whom ye also are builded together for an habitation of God through the Spirit* (Ephesians 2:11-13, 19-22).

THE FATHER AS HEAD OF THE HOUSE

The father remained the head of the house in New Testament times. As in the Old Testament, the father led the family, and each house was identified by reference to the father. When the rich man in Hades asked Abraham for a warning to his brothers, he asked him to send someone to his father's house (Luke 16:27). Hebrews describes Noah as having saved his house by building the ark (Hebrews 11:7).

The father was the spiritual leader of the house. When the prison keeper asked Paul and Silas what he must do to be saved, they told him, "Believe on the Lord Jesus Christ, and thou shalt be saved, and thy house" (Acts 16:31). As a result of his seeking salvation, Paul and Silas "spake unto him the word of the Lord, and to all that were in his house," and he and his household were baptized (Acts 16:32-33).

There were other instances of whole households believing at once, reported in Acts 18:8 and 1 Corinthians 1:16, although not necessarily as the result of the leadership of the patriarch. Lydia's household was baptized when she was baptized (Acts 16:15). Another example of guidance of the patriarch, however, is Cornelius, the centurion of the Italian Regiment, who gave alms generously and prayed regularly. Acts reports that he "feared God with all his house" (Acts 10:2). He invited Peter to preach to his household, as directed by the Lord (Acts 10:3-33). Peter preached to that household that whoever believes in Jesus will receive remission of sins, and "the Holy Ghost fell on all them which heard the word" (Acts 10:44).

GOD THE FATHER AS HEAD OF THE HOUSE OF GOD

Jesus called God not only His Father, but also the Father of those to whom He spoke. He did it several times in the Sermon on the Mount. The best-known example is His directive in the Lord's Prayer: we are to pray to God as "our Father." Matthew 6:9. He also spoke repeatedly in the Sermon on the Mount of "your Father in heaven" and "your heavenly Father."

Later, when He sent out the twelve, He told them not to fear those who kill the body but cannot kill the soul because one sparrow "shall not fall on the ground without your Father" (Matthew 10:28-29). He said, "Then shall the righteous shine forth as the sun in the kingdom of their Father" (Matthew 13:43). He even went so far as to say, "Call no man your father upon the earth: for one is your Father, which is in heaven" (Matthew 23:9). He told Mary Magdalene outside the tomb, "I ascend unto My Father, and your Father; and to my God, and your God" (John 20:17).

Paul described our hearts as crying out to God, "Abba, Father" (Romans 8:15; Galatians 4:6). He started each letter except Galatians, Second Timothy, and Titus with a benediction summoning grace and peace from "God our Father" (Romans 1:7; 1 Corinthians 1:3; 2 Corinthians 1:2; Ephesians 1:2; Philippians 1:2; Colossians 1:2; 1 Thessalonians 1:1; 2 Thessalonians 1:1; 1 Timothy 1:2; Philemon 3). In the other three letters, the benediction referred to "God the Father" (Galatians 1:3; 2 Timothy 1:2; Titus 1:4).

James said, "Bless we God, even the Father" (James 3:9). John referred to God as our Father several times in his First and Second Epistles.

Jesus, Paul, and James were expressing a well-established understanding of God, as the preceding chapter's examination of the Old Testament shows. The Pharisees claimed to Jesus, "We have one Father, even God" (John 8:41).

As our Father, God loves us. John said, "Behold, what manner of love the Father hath bestowed upon us, that we should be called the sons of God" (1 John 3:1). His love is the personal and attentive love a father shows his child. Jesus told us, "Your Father knoweth what things ye have need of, before ye ask him" (Matthew 6:8). Peter wrote of, "God the Father . . . which according to His abundant mercy hath begotten us again . . . to an inheritance . . . reserved in heaven for you" (1 Peter 1: 2-4). Peter told us that our Father cares for us and advised: "casting all your care upon him" (1 Peter 5:7).

As our Father, God provides for us. Jesus taught, "Take no thought, saying, What shall we eat? or, What shall we drink? or, Wherewithal shall we be clothed . . . for your heavenly Father knoweth that ye have need of all these things" (Matthew 6:31-32). Beyond providing food and clothing, Jesus also taught that "Your Father which is in heaven [will] give good things to them that ask him" (Matthew 7:11). Paul said, "God our Father ... hath blessed us with all spiritual blessings" (Ephesians 1:2-3). James said, "Every good gift and every perfect gift is from above, and cometh down from the Father of lights, with whom is no variableness, neither shadow of turning" (James 1:17).

As our Father, God rewards us for proper behavior. In the Sermon on the Mount, Jesus told the people that if they did charitable deeds in secret, prayed in secret, and fasted in secret, "thy Father which seeth in secret himself shall reward thee openly" (Matthew 6:4, 6, 18). He also told them that if they forgave men their trespasses, "Your heavenly Father will also forgive you" (Matthew 6:14).

As our Father, God chastens us when we do not follow His leading. Hebrews says, "If ye endure chastening, God dealeth with you as with sons; for what son is he whom the father chasteneth not?" (Hebrews 12:7)

6

NEW TESTAMENT MEMBERS

CHILDREN OF GOD

The word *house* in the New and the Old Testaments can refer to a household as an economic unit. In that case, servants and slaves are members of the house, in addition to people related to the father by blood or marriage. However, the role of God as Father is that of a father to His children, not that of a patriarch to his servants and slaves.

In the New Testament, people became children of God by being born again. Jesus told Nicodemus, "Except a man be born again, he cannot see the kingdom of God" (John 3:3). Peter wrote of being born again of God the Father to an inheritance reserved in heaven: "Blessed be the God and Father of our Lord Jesus Christ, which according to his abundant mercy hath begotten us again ... to an inheritance incorruptible ... reserved in heaven for you" (1 Peter 1:3-4).

Later, he spoke of "Being born again, not of corruptible seed, but of incorruptible, by the word of God" (1 Peter 1:23). James Montgomery Boice elaborated on incorruptible seed as follows:

> When Peter mentioned "seed," he was not talking about the kind of seeds we plant in the ground. He was referring to human semen, and was suggesting that God engenders spir-

itual children much like a human father engenders a human child.[7]

Peter then instructed, "As newborn babes, desire the sincere milk of the word, that ye may grow thereby," and went on to use the metaphor of a house, saying, "Ye also, as lively stones, are built up a spiritual house, an holy priesthood" (1 Peter 2:5).

In his Gospel, John said those who "become the sons of God" are "born, not of blood, nor of the will of the flesh, nor of the will of man, but of God" (John 1:12-13). John also wrote of being born of God in John 1; 3:9; 4:7; 5:1, 4, 18.

James wrote of being born of God:

Of His own will begat he us with the word of truth, that we should be a kind of firstfruits of his creatures (James 1:18).

Even children of Israel need to be born again. Nicodemus was a Jew (John 3:1), and Peter wrote to the dispersed Jews (1 Peter 1:1). When the Pharisees claimed that God was their Father, Jesus answered, "If God were your Father, ye would love me … Ye are of your father the devil" (John 8:42, 44).

Jesus preached in the Sermon on the Mount that the children of God are the peacemakers. Matthew 5: 9. Later, in the same sermon, He again said that the Father's children in heaven are those who love their enemies. (Matthew 5:44-45). John said that love is a characteristic of those born of God (1 John 4:7).

Paul told the Philippians that the sons of God are harmless and blameless and shine as lights in the world (Philippians 2:15). He told the Ephesians that God chose his children "that we should be holy and without blame before him in love" (Ephesians 1:4-5). John said that those who are born of God

---

[7] James Montgomery Boice, *Standing on the Rock*, Living Studies, p. 39.

keep themselves so that the wicked one does not touch them (1 John 5:18). John said that everyone has sin (1 John 1:8) but directed us not to commit sin (1 John 3:4).

Nicodemus asked Jesus twice how a man can be born again. John 3:4, 9. Jesus answered that He spoke of being "born of the Spirit" (John 3:5-8). Paul explained that people become children of God through faith in Christ Jesus (Galatians 3:26). He told the Romans, "For as many as are led by the Spirit of God, they are the sons of God" (Romans 8:14).

Paul has described that process as adoption. He said, "For ye have not received the spirit of bondage again to fear; but ye have received the Spirit of adoption, whereby we cry, Abba, Father" (Romans 8:15). We are predestined to adoption (Ephesians 1:5). In one sense, adoption occurs at the redemption of our bodies. Paul said to the Romans, "The earnest expectation of the creation waiteth for the manifestation of the sons of God . . . even we ourselves groan within ourselves, waiting for the adoption, to wit, the redemption of our body" (Romans 8:19, 23). In another sense, it occurs when we are born again. Paul said to the Galatians, "God sent forth his Son, made of a woman, made under the law, to redeem them that were under the law, that we might receive the adoption of sons" (Galatians 4:4-5).

As children of God, our behavior reflects on God. Jesus said, "Let your light so shine before men, that they may see your good works, and glorify your Father which is in heaven" (Matthew 5:16). In the first chapter of his first epistle, Peter directed the dispersed Jews to act "as obedient children, not fashioning yourselves according to the former lusts" (1 Peter 1:14). He continued in the second chapter: "abstain from fleshly lusts, which war against the soul; having your conversation honest among the Gentiles: that, whereas they speak against you as evildoers, they may by your good works, which they shall behold, glorify God in the day of visitation" (1 Peter 2:11-12).

THE INHERITANCE

As children of God, we are heirs of God. Paul told believers, "We are the children of God: and if children, then heirs; heirs of God, and joint-heirs with Christ" (Romans 8:16-17). Again, he told believers, "Thou art no more a servant, but a son; and if a son, then an heir of God through Christ" (Galatians 4:7).

The inheritance is the one promised to Abraham (Galatians 3:18, 29). Although the New Testament looks back to the promise of the legacy of the land as a historical event (Acts 7:5; Hebrews 11:8-9), it primarily looks ahead to the promise of inheriting everlasting life. "This is the promise," John tells us, "that he hath promised us, even eternal life" (1 John 2:25). The inheritance is salvation (Hebrews 1:14). It is described as eternal (Hebrews 9:15). It is incorruptible, undefiled, and reserved for us in heaven (1 Peter 1:4). Jesus said those who left houses, land, or family for His sake would inherit everlasting life (Matthew 19:29). Jews of Jesus' day took the promise seriously enough to ask Jesus what they needed to do to inherit eternal life (Luke 10:25; 18:18; and Mark 10:17).

Paul said, "Ye were sealed with that holy Spirit of promise, which is the earnest [guarantee] of our inheritance until the redemption of the purchased possession" (Ephesians 1:13-14). Similarly, when Jesus promised the inheritance of eternal life, He spoke of what would happen "in the regeneration when the Son of man shall sit in the throne of his glory" (Matthew 19:28).

Jesus also spoke of inheriting the kingdom of God (Matthew 25:34), as did Paul (1 Corinthians 6:9, 15:50; Galatians 5:21; Ephesians 5:5) and James (James 2:5).

Paul warned that "the unrighteous shall not inherit the kingdom of God" (1 Corinthians 6:9). In 1 Corinthians, he listed several types of unrighteous behavior (1 Corinthians 6:9-10). In Galatians 5:19-21, he added more, and in Ephesians 5:4, he including foolish talking. That extensive list would discourage anyone from hoping for an inheritance in God's house. After all, everyone is guilty of at least some of the behaviors on the list. Paul stressed this in Romans 2:1, "Wherein thou judgest another, thou condemnest thyself; for thou that judgest doest the same things." Our Father has provided a solution for His children by paying the price for those sins through Jesus' sacrificial death on the cross. At the end of the list in Corinthians, Paul said, "but ye are washed, but ye are sanctified, but ye are justified in the name of the Lord Jesus, and by the Spirit of our God" (1 Corinthians 6:11).

WAITING ON THE LORD

Because the full realization of that inheritance lies in the future, we must wait on the Lord.

Paul told the Romans, "Even we ourselves groan within ourselves, waiting for the adoption, to wit, the redemption of our body . . . we with patience wait for it" (Romans 8:23-25).

The author of Hebrews exhorted the readers to "be . . . followers of them who through faith and patience inherit the promises" (Hebrews 6:12).

In Luke 15:11-12, Luke quoted Jesus' story of a son who was not patient, asked for his inheritance in advance, and suffered by squandering it.

In contrast, Matthew tells of Jesus' parable (Matthew 25:1-13) of wedding guests who waited well for the bridegroom by being prepared with sufficient oil for their lamps. "They that were ready went in with him to the marriage: and the door was shut" (Matthew 25:10).

BROTHERS AND SISTERS

As children of God, we are brothers and sisters to Jesus, the Son of God. According to Hebrews, "both he that sanctifieth and they who are sanctified are all of one: for which cause he is not ashamed to call them brethren, saying, I will declare thy name unto my brethren, in the midst of the church will I sing praise unto thee" (Hebrews 2:11-12).

Paul said, "For whom he did foreknow, he also did predestinate to be conformed to the image of his Son, that he might be the firstborn among many brethren" (Romans 8:29).

Jesus is characterized as the firstborn to recognize his supreme status in that sibling relationship. In Colossians, Paul calls Jesus "the image of the invisible God, the firstborn of every creature" (Colossians 1:15). Hebrews calls Him the firstborn in describing His superiority over the angels:

For unto which of the angels said he at any time: Thou art my Son, this day have I begotten thee? And again, I will be to him a Father, and he shall be to me a Son? And again, when he bringeth in the firstbegotten into the world, he saith, And let all the angels of God worship him (Hebrews 1:5-6).

Paul said we are "heirs of God and joint-heirs with Christ" (Romans 8:17). Hebrews describes the joint-heirship as Jesus' inheriting everything (Hebrews 1:2) and upon His death, our inheriting from Him (Hebrews 9:16). The same image is expressed in the third chapter of Hebrews, which describes Jesus as "a son over his own house" (Hebrews 3:6).

As a child of God, each of us is a brother or sister to the other children of God. Before approaching our Father, we must have our relationships with our brothers and sisters in order. Jesus said, "If thou bring thy gift to the altar, and there rememberest that thy brother hath ought against thee; leave there thy gift before the altar, and go thy way; first be reconciled to thy brother, and then come and offer thy gift" (Matthew 5:23-24). John said, "He that loveth not his brother whom he hath seen, how can he love God whom he hath not seen?" (1 John 4:20)

Peter directed us, as "obedient children," to have "unfeigned love of the brethren" and to "see that ye love one another with a pure heart fervently" (1 Peter 1:14, 22). He said while we should "honor all men," we should "love the brotherhood" (1 Peter 2:17).

When we complain about the behavior of others, we act like typical brothers and sisters, but not like the brothers and sisters our Father would have us be. We behave like the brother Jesus described who was angry when his father celebrated the return of his wayward brother who had "devoured [the father's] living with harlots." The father responded, "Son, ... it was meet that we should make merry, and be glad: for this thy brother was dead, and is alive again; and was lost, and is found" (Luke 15:28-32).

Jesus challenged us to be better brothers and sisters, saying:

Judge not, that ye be not judged. For with what judgment ye judge, ye shall be judged: and with what measure ye mete, it shall be measured to you again. And why beholdest thou the mote that is in thy brother's eye, but considerest not the beam that is in thine own eye? Or how wilt thou say to thy brother, Let me pull out the mote out of thine eye; and behold, a beam is in thine own eye? Thou hypocrite, first cast out the beam out of thine own eye; and then shalt thou see clearly to cast out the mote out of thy brother's eye (Matthew 7:1-5).

James and Paul repeated Jesus' admonishment against judging our brothers and instructed us to look instead to our own behavior. James warned: "Grudge not one against another, brethren, lest ye be condemned: behold, the judge standeth before the door" (James 5:9). Paul wrote to the Romans:

But why dost thou judge thy brother? Or why dost thou set at nought thy brother? For we shall all stand before the judgment seat of Christ . . . Let us not therefore judge one another any more: but judge this rather, that no man put a stumblingblock or an occasion to fall in his brother's way (Romans 14:10, 13).

We do need to consider our brother's behavior to ensure he does not become a stumbling block for us. Paul told the Corinthians "not to keep company, if any man that is called a brother be a fornicator, or covetous, or an idolator, or a railer, or a drunkard, or an extortioner; with such an one no not to eat" (1 Corinthians 5:11). Similarly, Paul told the Thessalonians to "withdraw yourselves from every brother that walketh disorderly" (2 Thessalonians 3:6).

In directing us to withdraw from disorderly brothers, Paul was repeating advice given in Proverbs:

He that walketh with wise men shall be wise: but a companion of fools shall be destroyed (Proverbs 13:20).

Make no friendship with an angry man; and with a furious man thou shalt not go: lest thou learn his ways, and get a snare to thy soul (Proverbs 22:24-25).

Be not among winebibbers; among riotous eaters of flesh: for the drunkard and the glutton shall come to poverty: and drowsiness shall clothe a man with rags (Proverbs 23:20-21).

Paul's purpose, as the purpose of those proverbs, was to avoid bad influences. Paul said, "Keep the feast, not with . . . the leaven of malice and wickedness; but with the unleavened bread of sincerity and truth" (1 Corinthians 5:8).

In considering withdrawing from a disorderly brother, we should remember our own shortcomings and take care not to set unreasonable standards. Jesus pointed out that He was not suitable company in the Pharisees' view, saying, "The Son of man is come eating and drinking, and ye say, 'Behold a gluttonous man, and a winebibber, a friend of publicans [tax collectors] and sinners!'" (Luke 7:34). The Pharisees shunned Jesus, believing they were in accord with Proverbs 23, but they avoided the only man to be without sin. Withdrawing from brothers must be done cautiously and sparingly. The event that instigated Paul to direct withdrawal in 1 Corinthians was the extreme offense of a man's having sex with his father's wife (1 Corinthians 5:1).

We should attack the problem of sin but should not attack our brothers. Paul warned, "If ye bite and devour one another, take heed that ye be not consumed one of another" (Galatians 5:15). Attacking the sin of others may seem corrective, but it is, in fact, destructive.

Instead of looking at the speck in our brother or sister's eye, we should focus on our own sin and its effect on others. We underestimate both the extent of our own corruption and its destructive influence on others. We do better to help others to sin less by sinning less ourselves, rather than by attacking them.

We must address the problem of sin humbly. Paul told Titus to remind the Cretans "to speak evil of no man, to be no brawlers, but gentle, shewing all meekness unto all men" (Titus

3:2). He told the Galatians to be gentle and supportive, no matter what the behavior:

> *Brethren, if a man be overtaken in a fault, ye which are spiritual, restore such an one in the spirit of meekness . . . Bear ye one another's burdens* (Galatians 6:1-2).

That requires telling our brothers about our own sins, and seeking their prayer for those problems, rather than telling them about their sins. That should encourage them to tell of their sins, and seek our prayer, in return. James said, "Who art thou that judgest another? . . . Confess your faults one to another, and pray one for another, that ye may be healed" (James 4:12; 5:16).

The way to change others' behavior is to set an example for them, not to engage in public debate about their behavior. Paul told the Ephesians to expose "the unfruitful works of darkness" (Ephesians 5:11), but not by speaking of them. He said, "It is a shame even to speak of those things which are done of them in secret" (Ephesians 5:12). Instead, "All things that are reproved are made manifest by the light" (Ephesians 5:13).

Our Father tells us what not to do about the sins of our brothers and sisters, why not to do it, and what to do instead. We are right to be distressed by evil, but we are instructed to attack our own sin, not the sin of others.

Those familial bonds among brothers and sisters and between the children and the father are bonds of love and trust that draw us all close together. As John described it:

> *Beloved, if God so loved us, we ought also to love one another. If we love one another, God dwelleth in us, and his love is perfected in us . . . God is love; and he that dwelleth in love dwelleth in God, and God in him . . . We love him, because he first loved us* (1 John 4:11-19).

Those of us who enjoy those bonds stand in awe of our omniscient and omnipotent Father. Still, we do not see Him as an abstraction from afar but rather as One with whom we have a relationship of intimacy.

William James, in *The Varieties of Religious Experience*, said this about perceiving God:

> God is the natural appellation, for us Christians at least, for the supreme reality, so I will call this higher part of the universe by the name of God. We and God have business with each other; and in opening ourselves to his influence our deepest destiny is fulfilled.[8]

James' observation reflects a distance between God and man, a great chasm that is bridged by understanding God as Father. James' mere sketch of God as a being is made whole and vivid by that understanding.

---

[8] William James, *The Varieties of Religious Experience*, The Modern Library, Random House, page 561.

7

BIBLICAL FATHERS

Understanding that the Bible characterizes God as our Father raises the question whether it provides positive examples of human fathers. Sadly, few exist.

In considering the concept of the father as the head of an extended family, we saw examples of solid leadership in Noah, Abraham, and David. Noah's relationship with God resulted in God's inviting onto the ark Noah's wife, his sons, and his sons' wives (Genesis 7:13). Abraham rescued Lot from the captivity of the four kings (Genesis 14:1-16). David rescued his wives and the wives and children of his men from the Amalekites (1 Samuel 30:1-18). But each of those heads of families, and most other fathers in the Old Testament, fell short in the intimate relationship of father to his children.

PATRIARCHS

Job, who was "perfect and upright" (Job 1:1), was a good father. We are told:

And it was so, when the days of their [his sons'] feasting were gone about [had run their course], that Job sent and sanctified them, and rose up early in the morning, and offered burnt offerings according to the number of them all: for Job said, It may be that my sons have sinned, and cursed God in their hearts. Thus did Job continually (Job 1:5).

Otherwise, however, the examples of fatherhood provided by human fathers in the Old Testament are overwhelmingly examples of poor fathering.

The most dramatic act of a father toward his son, Abraham's presenting Isaac as an offering to the Lord, is not the act of poor fathering some might think it to be. It was a heart-wrenching act of obedience to the Lord and, at the same time, was not lacking in love toward Isaac, especially given Abraham's faith that "God was able to raise him up, even from the dead" (Hebrews 11:19). It is a model of God's sacrifice of His own Son, but beyond that, tells us nothing about fatherhood because of its singularity.

That singularity, and the resulting difficulty in drawing lessons from it, is described by Soren Kierkegaard:

> Abraham I cannot understand, in a certain sense there is nothing I can learn from him but astonishment. If people fancy that by considering the outcome of this story they might let themselves be moved to believe, they deceive themselves and want to swindle God out of the first movement of faith, the infinite resignation. They would suck worldly wisdom out of the paradox.[9]

The relationship that Abraham had with his other son, Ishmael, went badly. It began with Abraham's waiting poorly for the Lord to fulfill His promise to give Abraham a son, and Abraham's taking the matter into his own hands by having a child with his wife's Egyptian maidservant, Hagar. It came to its inevitable end when Abraham reluctantly placated Sarah at God's direction by sending Hagar and Ishmael away.

---

[9] Soren Kierkegaard *Fear and Trembling*, Princeton University Press 1968 edition, page 48.

Before Abraham, the one reported incident between Noah and his sons was an unfortunate one, due to Noah's misbehavior. Noah got drunk and lay uncovered in his tent. He set up his son Ham to sin in telling his brothers about his father's shame. It was also an embarrassment for his other sons, who had to take care to cover him while walking backward so as not to look on his nakedness (Genesis 9:20-27).

Noah's nakedness before his sons paled in comparison to Lot's shameful behavior with his daughters. Lot's relationship with his daughters was so bad that Lot offered his daughters to the lascivious mob in Sodom in place of his two guests (Genesis 19:1-11). His daughters later got him drunk and became pregnant by him (Genesis 19:30-38).

Isaac favored his son Esau over his other son Jacob (Genesis 25:28). Isaac was repaid by Jacob's tricking him to get Esau's blessing, in conspiracy with Rebekah, Isaac's wife and the boys' mother (Genesis 27:1-40).

Jacob learned nothing from his resentment of his father's favoritism other than how to misbehave himself. Jacob repeated Isaac's example, favoring his son Joseph over his other sons (Genesis 37:3). That caused murderous dissension among his other sons, greatly hurting Joseph, and bringing great grief upon Jacob.

PRIESTS AND JUDGES

Aaron, the first in the line of priests from the house of Levi, failed to the extent that two of his four sons abused their priestly roles. After Aaron and his sons were consecrated as priests, they placed an offering on the altar, and "the glory of the Lord appeared unto all the people, and there came a fire out from before the Lord, and consumed upon the altar the burnt offering and the fat" (Leviticus 9:23-24). The people were overwhelmed. They shouted and fell prostrate. Nadab and Abihu responded with a presumptuous act:

> *And Nadab and Abihu, the sons of Aaron, took either of them his censer, and put fire therein, and put incense thereon, and offered strange fire before the Lord, which he commanded them not. And there went out fire from the Lord, and devoured them, and they died before the Lord* (Leviticus 10:1-2).

Moses relayed to Aaron the Lord's explanation: "I will be sanctified in them that come nigh me" (Leviticus 10:3).

Moses then became angry at Aaron's other two sons, Eleazar and Ithamar, for not eating the sin offering as he had instructed, and Aaron defended them (Leviticus 10:12-20). The extent of Aaron's culpability in the errors of his sons is not described in Scripture, although it notes Aaron's failure as a leader of the children of Israel. While Moses was receiving the Ten Commandments from the Lord, they made a golden calf, and Aaron did not restrain them, "unto their shame among their enemies" (Exodus 32:25).

Gideon failed in both his role as patriarch and in his father-son relationship with Abimelech. The people asked Gideon, "Rule thou over us, both thou, and thy son, and thy son's son also: for thou hast delivered us from the hand of Midian" (Judges 8:22).

Gideon correctly answered, "I will not rule over you, neither shall my son rule over you: the Lord shall rule over you" (Judges 8:23). However, he failed to get his son, Abimelech, to join in that resolve. Gideon secured neither Abimelech's agreement nor his obedience. Also, he asked the people for their gold to make an ephod from it, which "became a snare unto Gideon, and to his house" (Judges 8:27).

When Gideon died, Abimelech killed his seventy brothers, except Jotham, the youngest, who hid. The men of Shechem then made Abimelech king (Judges 9:5-6). Gideon's having more than seventy sons gave him a large house but impaired his ability to have an intimate paternal relationship with any of them.

Like Aaron's sons, Nadab and Abihu, Eli's sons also sinned as priests. They did not know the Lord and were corrupt (1 Samuel 2:12). They abused their role as priests by using sacrifices as food and lying with the women who assembled at the door of the tabernacle of meeting (1 Samuel 2:13-17, 22).

Eli spoke to them about it, saying, "It is no good report that I hear: ye make the Lord's people to transgress" (1 Samuel 2:24). The Lord considered that to be inadequate and blamed Eli for his sons' behavior, saying, "Wherefore . . . honourest thy sons above me?" (1 Samuel 2:29) Therefore, the Lord moved the priesthood from Eli's house to Samuel's (1 Samuel 2:30-36).

Despite the Lord's moving the priesthood to Samuel's house because Eli failed in rearing his sons, Samuel failed in rearing his sons too. His sons "walked not in his ways" but instead "turned aside after lucre, and took bribes, and perverted judgment" (1 Samuel 8:3). Those were not the "sins against the Lord" that Eli said his sons were guilty of (1 Samuel 2:25). When the people rejected Samuel's setting up his sons as judges and demanded that he "make us a king to judge us like all the nations" (1 Samuel 8:1-5), the Lord did not hold Samuel accountable. Instead, the Lord told Samuel, "They have not rejected thee, but they have rejected me, that I should not reign over them" 1 (Samuel 8:7). Even so, Samuel behaved poorly as a father.

KINGS

In response to the people's demand for a king, Samuel anointed Saul as king at the instruction of the Lord (1 Samuel 9:16). Saul, the first king of Israel, treated his son Jonathan outrageously. As he sat with Jonathan at the table to eat the feast of the New Moon, Saul became so angry with Jonathan over his friendship with David that he called him a "son of a perverse rebellious woman" (1 Samuel 20:30) and "cast a javelin at him to smite him" (1 Samuel 20:33).

David, the second king of Israel, loved his sons. He was distraught over the illness of his first child with Bathsheba (2 Samuel 12:16-20). He wept at the death of his rebellious son Absalom (2 Samuel 18:33). But that love did not make him a good father.

David was overly lenient with both Absalom and Adonijah. As to Absalom, David instructed Joab to "deal gently for my sake with the young man," even though Absalom was leading a rebellion against David (2 Samuel 18:5). Adonijah conspired to rule in place of Solomon, his father's choice to succeed him. First Kings 1:5-6 reports, "Then Adonijah ... exalted himself, saying, I will be king ... And his father had not displeased [rebuked] him at any time in saying, Why hast thou done so?"

David's political problems with Absalom and Adonijah alone would have set David apart as a poor father, but David's family suffered from other terrible behavior among the children. Another of David's sons, Amnon, raped his sister, Tamar (2 Samuel 13:1-19). Absalom then murdered Amnon for the crime (2 Samuel 13:23-29).

Solomon did succeed David, despite Adonijah's attempt to gain the throne. Solomon also had a rebellious son. Solomon's son Rehoboam, his successor, showed disrespect to his deceased father. He told the people, "My father made your yoke heavy, and I will add to your yoke: my father also chastised you with whips, but I will chastise you with scorpions" (1 Kings 12:14). As a result, the kingdom split between Israel and Judah. Despite the excellent advice on fathering attributed to Solomon in Proverbs, Solomon earned his son's disrespect.

In the generations that followed, until both Israel and Judah were taken into captivity, with a few exceptions, the kings of both Israel and Judah passed down to their sons a tradition of evil. One example is Amon, King of Judah, described in the following passage:

And he did that which was evil in the sight of the Lord, as his father Manasseh did. And he walked in all the way that his father walked in; and served the idols that his father served, and worshiped them (2 Kings 21:20-21).

SUMMARY

Overall, the Old Testament fathers related poorly to their sons. The sons suffered as a result and typically passed on the pattern of substandard behavior and deficient fathering to their sons. Those relationships cannot serve as a model of our relationship with God but rather serve as a stark contrast to God's role as a father.

The primary pattern of behavior we can see in the Old Testament is not merely contrary to God's character. We often prefer it to God's behavior. Most of us would agree that it is inadequate fathering, but as children, we would like to find it in our fathers because we believe it would make our lives as children easier.

Noah and Lot failed to exercise adequate self-discipline.

We can see how Noah's self-indulgence hurt Ham, but it pleased Ham on some level since he shared it with his brothers rather than acting to cure it as his brothers did. In that awful encounter in Sodom, Lot's daughters presumably wished for a stronger, more protective father. Later, however, Lot's weakness enabled them to get what they wanted, despite its reprehensibility.

Aaron, Eli, Samuel, and David failed to exercise adequate discipline over their sons. Their sons enjoyed that leniency, at least for a time, happily doing as they pleased. As outside observers, we can see how that hurt them, but they could not see it. That blinding effect of the drive toward self-indulgence is why fathers must consistently exercise discipline over their children.

Human fatherhood is not devoid of effective discipline, notwithstanding the Old Testament examples. We know what fatherhood should be, and describing God as our Father helps us understand God's role as the head of His family and His relationship with each family member. The specific examples of the father-child relationship in the Old Testament do not help us know God by serving as a model of His relationship with us. Still, they help us understand God by showing us the consequences of poor fathering and the need for His sometimes painful fathering.

8

BIBLICAL SIBLINGS

Similar to examining fatherhood, understanding that the children of God are siblings to each other raises the question of whether the Bible presents positive examples of sibling relationships. Again, with a few exceptions, human beings fall short.

The Old Testament is a sad history of one poor sibling relationship after another. It takes eight verses after the fall for a man to kill his brother. The first big brother, Cain, murdered his younger brother, Abel, out of resentment because God favored Abel's offering over Cain's (Genesis 4:8).

Two chapters later, the next family to gain biblical attention is Noah's family. Of Noah's three sons, Shem and Japheth reacted appropriately to Noah's passing out naked from drunkenness, and Ham did not, but no hostility among the brothers over that incident is reported (Genesis 9:20-27).

Two chapters after the history of Noah's family, the Bible introduces Abraham, and brotherly friction returns. Abraham had two sons, and the older brother, Ishmael, mocked his little brother, Isaac, when Abraham held a feast in Isaac's honor the same day Isaac was weaned (Genesis 21:8-9). Isaac's son Jacob was only seconds younger than his twin brother Esau, but Esau still deserved the birthright. When a famished Esau begged pottage from Jacob, Jacob shared it only in return for the birthright (Genesis 25:29-34). Later, Jacob cheated his brother out of his father's blessing (Genesis 27). Esau then plotted to kill Jacob (Genesis 27:41), although the brothers later reconciled (Genesis 33:3-4).

The sibling contention extended into the third generation of Abraham's descendants when Jacob's son Joseph incurred the hatred of his brothers, who plotted to kill him. However, Reuben convinced them to sell him into slavery instead (Genesis 37). Eventually, in Egypt, they reconciled (Genesis 45:15).

In the collaboration between Moses and Aaron, a break occurred in the string of bad relations between brothers (Exodus 4-40). They suffered a setback over Aaron's role in making the golden calf (Exodus 32:21-22), but that was a single (though severe) incident from which their relationship recovered.

Sibling friction recurs with Jesse's family. The oldest of Jesse's sons, Eliab, angrily accused his youngest brother, David, of pride and insolence for going to the camp of the army and saying to Goliath, "Who is this uncircumcised Philistine, that he should defy the armies of the living God?" (1 Samuel 17:26-29) Even though the accusation was wrong, it was a slight insult compared to the terrible crimes committed among David's children. The oldest brother, Amnon, raped his sister Tamar (2 Samuel 13:1-20), and their brother Absalom killed Amnon (2 Samuel 13:28-29).

Through all that strife, some examples of brotherhood stand out in the reconciliations of Esau and Jacob and of Joseph and his brothers.

Jacob sent messengers to Esau, who reported to Jacob, "He cometh to meet thee, and four hundred men with him."

Genesis states, "Then Jacob was greatly afraid and distressed . . ." Jacob said, O God of my father Abraham, and God of my father Isaac . . . I am not worthy of the least of all the mercies . . . which thou hast shewed unto thy servant . . . Deliver me, I pray thee . . . from the hand of Esau: for I fear him . . . And Esau ran to meet him, and embraced him, and fell on his neck and kissed him: and they wept" (Genesis 32:6-7; 9-11; 33:4).

The reconciliation of Joseph with his brothers is similar. Despite his brothers' evil behavior toward him, Joseph forgave them. He also tried to clear their guilt, saying, "Be not grieved, nor angry with yourselves, that ye sold me hither: for God did send me before you to preserve life . . . So now it was not you that sent me hither, but God" (Genesis 45:5, 8). Then, Genesis reports, "He fell upon his brother Benjamin's neck, and wept; and Benjamin wept upon his neck. Moreover he kissed all his brethren, and wept upon them: and after that his brethren talked with him" (Genesis 45:14-15).

In the New Testament, the reported sibling relationships went better. Two sets of brothers, Simon and Andrew and James and John, left their work as fishermen to follow Jesus (Matthew 4:18-22; Mark 1:16-20). Although Martha criticized her sister, Mary, for sitting at Jesus' feet to hear Jesus' teaching while Martha served (Luke 10:38-41), they seemed close to each other. Jesus loved them and their brother, Lazarus (John 11:5) to the point of weeping with Mary over Lazarus' death (John 11:32-35).

However, Jesus used sibling rivalry to illustrate relationships in the house of God. The parable of the lost son, also known as the parable of the prodigal son, primarily demonstrates the father's love, forgiveness, and grace toward his younger son. The latter took his inheritance and squandered it on riotous living before returning to his father's house. But it also features a poor sibling reaction, which should be a cautionary example. Upon hearing of the celebratory feast arranged by the father, the older brother became angry and refused to participate (Luke 15:11-31). The father explained, "It was meet that we should make merry, and be glad: for this thy brother was dead, and is alive again; and was lost, and is found" (Luke 15:32).

In the house of God, we should respect and emulate God the Father by having love and support for our brothers and sisters, not competitiveness that produces envy and resentment.

9

OLD TESTAMENT SON, DAVID

Much as the fathers discussed in the Biblical Fathers chapter failed in their roles as fathers, Ham, Lot's daughters, Jacob, Nadab, Abihu, Abimelech, Eli's sons, Samuel's sons, Amnon, Absalom, Adonijah, and Rehoboam, among others, failed in their responsibilities as children. Those father-son and father-daughter relationships serve as cautionary warnings rather than models. No details are provided in Scripture regarding the relationships of those children with their heavenly Father. First Samuel tells us that Eli's sons did not know the Lord (1 Samuel 2:13-17), but for the rest, we can only draw inferences about their relationships with the Lord.

However, the Old Testament is rich with detail on David's relationship with the Lord. Examining that information reveals much about God as our Father and about proper and improper behavior as a child of God.

DAVID'S NATURAL FAMILY

David had a close, loving relationship with a surrogate brother, Jonathan. After learning of Jonathan's death, David said, "I am distressed for thee, my brother Jonathan: very pleasant hast thou been unto me: thy love to me was wonderful, passing the love of women" (2 Samuel 1:26).

In contrast to that relationship, in the one reported interaction between David and a natural brother, his brother Eliab scolded him for leaving their father's sheep to go to the battlefield, even though their father had asked David to do it. Eliab wrongly accused David of pride and insolence (1 Samuel 17:28). David honored relationships with his extended family by choosing a nephew, Joab, to be commander of his armies, although that relationship deteriorated.

The relationships of David's children with each other and their father were as bad as they could be. Among David's children, one brother, Amnon, raped a sister, Tamar (2 Samuel 13:1-19). Another brother, Absalom, murdered him for it (2 Samuel 13:23-29). Absalom "stole the hearts of the men of Israel" from David (2 Samuel 15:6) and led a rebellion against him. Later, as David neared death, Adonijah (with the help of Joab) conspired to become king upon his father's death in place of Solomon, his father's choice.

David was a loving father. When his first child by Bathsheba was dying, he pleaded with God for the child, fasted, and spent the nights lying on the ground for seven days (2 Samuel 12:16-20). When Absalom rebelled against him, he instructed Joab to "deal gently for my sake with the young man" (2 Samuel 18:5). When Joab nonetheless killed Absalom, David wept, saying, "O my son Absalom, my son, my son Absalom! Would God I had died for thee, O Absalom, my son, my son!" (2 Samuel 18:33)

As his tolerance of Absalom's rebellion shows, David failed to provide discipline to his children. First Kings explains Adonijah's conspiracy by noting that "His father had not displeased him at any time in saying, Why hast thou done so?" (1 Kings 1:6)

We are told little about David's relationship with his natural father, Jesse, other than that David tended his father's sheep and took grain and bread to his brothers on the battlefield at his father's direction.

We learn more from David's relationship with his spiritual Father. The Bible provides a detailed description of David's relationship to God in terms of David's carrying out his role as a member of the household. We can better understand our roles as children of God by observing David's experience.

DAVID AS A YOUTH

David's dramatic act in the service of the Lord in his youth was his defeat of Goliath. A common conception of that event is that David was an adolescent boy, armed with a sling that was little more than a toy. Under those circumstances, Goliath would have been felled only by miraculous intervention by the Lord.

However, David was a mighty warrior in his own right, though inexperienced, and his sling was a deadly weapon of war. Consequently, God-given human skills brought down Goliath, rather than a God-sent miracle. Understanding that helps us better understand David's relationship with God.

David began fighting for the Lord as a youth, facing Goliath. Saul described David's youthfulness when he said, "Thou art not able to go against this Philistine to fight with him: for thou art but a youth, and he a man of war from his youth" (1 Samuel 17:33). The King James Version of 1 Samuel 17:56 quotes Saul, in talking to Abner, as calling David a "stripling," which is an adolescent boy. However, the Hebrew word is better translated as "young man." Youth is relative. A nineteen-year-old Marine is a youth from the perspective of a fifty-five-year-old man but is a warrior to be reckoned with.

Saul said Goliath had been a "man of war from his youth." He started being a man of war while still in his youth. It was a mismatch because of Goliath's experience, not because a youth could not be a man of war.

A servant of Saul had described David as "a mighty valiant man, and a man of war" (1 Samuel 16:18).

Saul was a big man, head and shoulders above the rest (1 Samuel 9:2). Even so, Saul offered David his armor (1 Samuel 17:38). That would have been preposterous if David had been a little boy. David rejected it because he had not tried it out, not because it was too large (1 Samuel 17:39).

So David was no little boy when he faced Goliath but a young man gifted in using the sling. Furthermore, contrary to the modern perception, the sling was no toy.

The Israelites' arsenal was limited. They had not yet entered the Iron Age, and the Philistines withheld the technology from them for military defense reasons. According to G. Herbert Livingston, "The Philistines had learned new methods of tempering iron from the Hittites and held a monopoly on the method for several hundred years."[10] The Bible reports that during the reign of King Saul, "Now there was no smith found throughout all the land of Israel: for the Philistines said, Lest the Hebrews make them swords or spears" (1 Samuel 13:19).

When Saul fought the Philistines near Michmash, he and Jonathan were the only Israelites with either sword or spear (1 Samuel 13:22). Instead of swords and spears, most of the soldiers used bows and slings. In the time of the judges, there were "seven hundred chosen men left-handed; every one could

---

[10] G. Herbert Livingston, *The Pentateuch in its Cultural Environment*, Baker Book House Company, 1974 edition, page 29.

sling stones at an hair breadth, and not miss" (Judges 20:16). The men with David at Ziklag were "armed with bows, and could use both the right hand and the left in hurling stones" (1 Chronicles 12:2).

When Moab rebelled against Israel, Israelite "slingers went about [Kir Haraseth], and smote it" (2 Kings 3:25). In the time of Uzziah, the army of Judah had spears but also used bows and slings (2 Chronicles 26:14). Zechariah prophesied, "The Lord of hosts shall defend them; and they shall devour, and subdue with sling stones" (Zechariah 9:15).

If you could sling a stone with deadly force at a hair and not miss, a sling was an ideal weapon to use against someone armed with a sword and a long spear, protected by armor and a shield, and who had a long reach and spear, like Goliath (1 Samuel 17:4, 6, 7, 45). Understanding that it was not a miracle that David killed Goliath with a sling helps us see that the event's significance is that David used skills given to him by God for the glory of God.

David did not expect a miracle. David "chose him five smooth stones out of the brook" (1 Samuel 17:40). If he had expected God to intervene miraculously, he would not have seen a need to be prepared to sling multiple stones. David understood that the means for defeating Goliath lay within himself.

David had confidence because his skills came from God. When Saul told David Goliath outmatched him, David told Saul, "The Lord that delivered me out of the paw of the lion, and out of the paw of the bear, he shall deliver me out of the hand of this Philistine" (1 Samuel 17:37). He announced to Goliath, "This day will the Lord deliver thee into mine hand" (1 Samuel 17:46).

David had confidence because the Lord had trained him

to use those skills. David answered Saul's argument that he was not as experienced as Goliath by explaining to Saul that his exploits with the lion and the bear had prepared him for confronting Goliath: "Thy servant slew both the lion and the bear: and this uncircumcised Philistine shall be as one of them" (1 Samuel 17:36).

David sang, "It is God that girdeth me with strength, and maketh my way perfect. He maketh my feet like hinds' feet … He teacheth my hands to war" (Psalm 18:32-34). Another time, he sang, "Blessed be the Lord my strength, which teacheth my hands to war, and my fingers to fight" (Psalm 144:1). And again, he sang, "He teacheth my hands to war; so that a bow of steel is broken by mine arms … thou hast girded me with strength to battle" (2 Samuel 22:35, 40).

Furthermore, David used those skills for the glory of God. He was eager to face Goliath because Goliath defied the armies of the living God. He expressed his outrage at that defiance both to the men of Israel and to Goliath himself (1 Samuel 17:26, 45). He wanted to fight and kill Goliath "in the name of the Lord of hosts" so that "all the earth may know that there is a God in Israel" (1 Samuel 17:45-46).

DAVID AS AN ADULT

David went on from his confrontation with Goliath to continue using his skills as a warrior and proved to be God's greatest warrior of that time, perhaps of any time. However, God's greatest warrior eventually used a surrogate in his place. When David used the gifts God gave him to perform his role in the household of God, then and only then did he prosper.

During the reign of Saul, David had great victories at Keilah and Ziklag after first inquiring of the Lord (1 Samuel

23:2; 30:8). When the Philistines attacked Keilah, robbing the threshing floors, David inquired of the Lord, and at the direction of the Lord, he struck the Philistines and saved Keilah (1 Samuel 23:1-5).

After Saul's death, David was in a civil war with Saul's son Ishbosheth and Saul's captain Abner. David acquired his own captain, Joab, who was David's nephew (2 Samuel 2:13, 18). Joab was a dangerous man. When Joab led David's army in battle at Gibeon against Ishbosheth's army, led by Abner, Joab's brother Asahel personally pursued Abner. Abner tried to persuade Asahel to go after someone else, knowing that he would have to answer to Joab if he killed Asahel. Abner said, "Turn thee aside from following me: wherefore should I smite thee to the ground? How then should I hold up my face to Joab thy brother?" (2 Samuel 2:22)

Asahel did not turn aside, and Abner killed him. Abner made peace with David. Joab sent for Abner, and "when Abner was returned to Hebron, Joab took him aside in the gate to speak with him quietly, and smote him there under the fifth rib, that he died, for the blood of Asahel his brother" (2 Samuel 3:27).

When Joab murdered Abner, David lamented Abner's death, saying, "Died Abner as a fool dieth?" (2 Samuel 3:33). David called Joab and his brother Abishai "too hard for me" (2 Samuel 3: 39). Nonetheless, he continued with Joab as his captain.

Second Samuel reports, "When the Philistines heard that they had anointed David king over Israel, all the Philistines came up to seek David" (2 Samuel 5:17). David again had great victories over the Philistines at Baal Perazim and in the Valley of Rephaim, after inquiring of the Lord (2 Samuel 5:19, 23; 1

Chronicles 14:10, 14). The text does not mention Joab; David's reliance was on the Lord.

David then prevailed in battle against the Philistines, the Moabites, and Hadadezer of Zobah and his Syrian allies. Throughout those campaigns, "the Lord preserved David whithersoever he went" (2 Samuel 8:6, 14; 1 Chronicles 18:6, 13).

When the time came to fight the Ammonites and the Syrians, David initially sent Joab. The Syrians fled from Joab and then regrouped. At that point, David went out to battle them and defeated them (2 Samuel 10; 1 Chronicles 19).

Following that, David sent Joab to besiege Rabbah, "but David tarried still at Jerusalem" (2 Samuel 11:1; 1 Chronicles 20:1). While tarrying instead of fighting, he arranged to have Uriah killed so he could marry Uriah's wife, Bathsheba. After successfully besieging Rabbah, Joab invited David to claim the victory, "lest I take the city, and it be called after my name" (2 Samuel 12:28). So David "went to Rabbah, and fought against it, and took it" (2 Samuel 12:29).

When David's son Absalom attempted to seize the throne, David sent out his army under the command of Joab, Abishai, and Ittai; David stayed behind (2 Samuel 18:4-5). David instructed them to "deal gently for my sake with the young man" (2 Samuel 18:5). However, Joab killed Absalom (2 Samuel 18:14) and Amasa, Absalom's captain (2 Samuel 20:10). Later, on his deathbed, David directed Solomon to avenge Abner and Amasa's deaths and "let not his hoar head go down to the grave in peace" (1 Kings 2:6).

In his contention with David, Joab was sometimes right. When Satan enticed David to number Israel (2 Samuel 24:1; 1 Chronicles 21:1), Joab urged David not to "be a cause of trespass to Israel" (1 Chronicles 21:3). David ignored Joab's advice, and Joab did as David directed, except that he did not count Levi and Benjamin because "the king's word was abominable to Joab" (1 Chronicles 21:6).

Although David had proclaimed that Solomon would succeed him, David's oldest living son, Adonijah, plotted to seize the throne, aided by Joab. However, the plot failed, and Solomon ordered Adonijah and Joab to be executed (1 Kings 2:12-34).

When David employed his skills with the guidance of the Lord, he prospered. When he relied on Joab, his authority suffered and his success diminished.

Choosing a captain was customary and appropriate. Saul had Abner. Absalom, in his revolt, had Amasa. Adonijah, in his revolt, had Joab. Delegating authority is a good thing. Moses' father-in-law gave Moses excellent advice to delegate. Jethro warned Moses, "Thou wilt surely wear away, both thou, and this people that is with thee: for this thing is too heavy for thee: thou art not able to perform it thyself alone" (Exodus 18:18). The only thing wrong with Jethro's advice was that he did not suggest enough people report to Moses. God corrected that by directing Moses to gather seventy elders to whom the other leaders would answer to "bear the burden of the people with thee" (Numbers 11:16-17).

But David did more than delegate some authority to Joab. Fighting was one of David's chief skills. One of Saul's servants described David as a "cunning player on an harp," "prudent in matters," and a "man of war" (1 Samuel 16:16, 18). To tell Joab to fight his battles was like telling someone else to play the harp in his place. As we saw when we looked at David and Goliath, God gave David the skills of a man of war to advance His purposes. Fighting the enemies of God was one of David's primary assignments from God.

Of course, David was king as well as warrior, carrying out another primary assignment as he "executed judgment and justice unto all his people" (2 Samuel 8:15). But in that time of militarily defending against the enemies of the Lord, going to battle was not inconsistent with acting as king. For example, King Saul died in battle (1 Samuel 31).

Abigail perceptively said of David, "The Lord will certainly make my lord a sure house; because my lord fighteth the battles of the Lord" (1 Samuel 25:28). Hebrews 11 gives specific examples of great faith, then summarizes David and others as people who, through faith, "out of weakness were made strong, waxed valiant in fight, turned to flight the armies of the aliens" (Hebrews 11:34).

David again took to the field in the final campaigns against the Philistines. Abishai had to come to his aid. By that time, David had aged and weakened and fell into danger because he grew faint in battle. His men said, "Thou shalt go no more out with us to battle, that thou quench not the light of Israel" (2 Samuel 21:15-17). That does not justify his sending Joab while still in his prime.

One result of David's abdication of that responsibility to Joab was that a man David called "too hard" performed a task in which life hung in the balance. When David and Joab's brother Abishai had Saul in their grasp, Abishai wanted to kill Saul, while David extended mercy because Saul was the Lord's anointed (1 Samuel 26). When David sent Joab in his place, men died that David would have spared.

Beyond that, however, David himself suffered by giving up vital opportunities to serve in the household of the Lord by using the gifts the Lord had given him. David prospered when he enthusiastically used those gifts for the Lord as a dutiful son. When he allowed them to languish, he slipped into sin.

Like the youthful David, as children of God, we should be eager to glorify God using the skills God gave us. We should be confident in using our skills, knowing they came from God. We should be diligent in training to use those skills. When lions attack our peaceful herds, we should remind ourselves that the Lord has sent them to train us. We should deal effectively with the problem at hand and appreciate the experience it provides. Knowing the training has prepared us, we should be confident using our skills for each new challenge.

We should use our skills to further God's purposes, and we should understand that their successful use glorifies God, not us. We should be confident in the use of those skills, knowing for whom they are being used.

When a difficult job arises for which we are specially gifted and thoroughly trained, we should not tell ourselves that we are needed elsewhere or that another member of God's household can do it just as well (or at least well enough). Unlike the older David, we should use our God-given skills to carry out the assignments He gives us at every opportunity. After a period of exemplary work on complicated tasks, we should not rest on our laurels. We should not decide that we have done enough and drop out of the fray.

10

DAVID'S VIEW OF THE HOUSE

Saul first encountered David not as a warrior but as a musician. Saul was tormented and sought a harp player to soothe him at his servants' suggestion (1 Samuel 16:14-17). One of Saul's servants suggested David. He reported to Saul that David was "a mighty valient man, and a man of war," but also that he was "cunning in playing," and "prudent in matters" (1 Samuel 16:18). We have fruits of those gifts with us today in the form of David's songs, many of which are in the Psalms. His songs richly describe the Lord's attributes, including those of the Lord as Father.

Some of David's songs directly refer to God as Father, to God's house, to the brotherhood of believers, or the inheritance.

GOD THE FATHER

Psalm 103 refers to God as Father and believers as children: "Like as a father pitieth his children, so the Lord pitieth them that fear him" (Psalms 103:13).

Similarly, Psalm 68 refers to God as Father: "A father of the fatherless . . . is God in his holy habitation" (Psalms 68:5).

Beyond the Psalms, David addressed God as Father when he blessed the Lord for the people's offerings for the building of the temple. He said: "Blessed be thou, Lord God of Israel our father, for ever and ever" (1 Chronicles 29:10).

GOD'S HOUSE

To David, dwelling in God's house means being in the presence of God to behold His beauty. It means receiving God's parental care and protection from danger and having access to God when we have questions.

One thing have I desired of the Lord, that will I seek after; that I may dwell in the House of the Lord all the days of my life, to behold the beauty of the Lord, and to enquire in his temple . . . When my father and my mother forsake me, then the Lord will take me up (Psalms 27:4, 10).

The children living in the house of God enjoy protection and abundant provision for their needs.

Therefore the children of men put their trust under the shadow of thy wings. They shall be abundantly satisfied with the fatness of thy house (Psalms 36:7-8).

Psalm 26 seems to refer to the tabernacle, with the Holy of Holies, where God's glory dwelt, but it also refers to inhabiting God's house:

Lord, I have loved the habitation of thine house, and the place where thine honour dwelleth (Psalms 26:8).

Psalm 15 identifies those who dwell in the house of the Lord:

Lord, who shall abide in thy tabernacle? Who shall dwell in thy holy hill? He that walketh uprightly, and worketh righteousness, and speaketh the truth in his heart. He that backbiteth not with his tongue, nor doeth evil to his neighbor, nor taketh up a reproach against his neighbor. In whose eyes a vile person is contemned; but he honoureth them that fear the Lord. He that sweareth to his own hurt, and changeth not. He that putteth not out his money to usury, nor taketh reward against the innocent.

He that doeth these things shall never be moved (Psalms 15:1-5).

Dwelling in the house of God brings the blessing of instruction on how to live to please God and the responsibility of living that way.

David's expectation, having entered the house of the Lord, was never to leave it.

Surely goodness and mercy shall follow me all the days of my life: and I will dwell in the house of the Lord for ever (Psalms 23:6).

I will abide in thy tabernacle for ever (Psalm 61:4).

The Hebrew text translated "for ever" more literally means "for the length of my days," so the suggestion of eternity is uncertain.

BROTHERS

Psalm 22 refers to believers as brothers:

I will declare thy name unto my brethren: in the midst of the congregation will I praise thee (Psalm 22:22).

Psalm 22 looks ahead to Jesus. Verse 16 says, "They pierced my hands and my feet." John 20:24-27 confirms the practice of crucifixion: Jesus' hands and feet were pierced when He was nailed to the cross. Psalms 22:18 says, "They part my garments among them, and cast lots upon my vesture." Matthew 27:35 and Mark 15:24 report that those who crucified Jesus divided His garments and cast lots for them. Matthew 27:46 and Mark 15:34 report that on the cross, Jesus quoted the first verse of Psalm 22, crying out, "My God, My God, why hast thou forsaken me?" In the sense that Psalm 22 speaks of Jesus, it describes believers as brothers of Jesus.

Psalm 133 also refers to believers as brothers:

Behold, how good and how pleasant it is for brethren to dwell together in unity! It is like the precious ointment upon the head, that ran down upon the beard, even Aaron's beard: that went down to the skirts of his garments; as the dew of Hermon, and as the dew that descended upon the mountains of Zion; for there the Lord commanded the blessing, even life for evermore (Psalms 133:1-3).

Those three verses are the entire psalm. The Psalm celebrates the unity of believers as brothers.

INHERITANCE

Psalm 37 speaks of waiting on the Lord and receiving the inheritance:

Rest in the Lord, and wait patiently for him: fret not thyself because of him who prospereth in his way, because of the man who bringeth wicked devices to pass . . . For evildoers shall be cut off: but those that wait upon the Lord, they shall inherit the earth . . . But the meek shall inherit the earth; and shall delight themselves in the abundance of peace . . . The Lord knoweth the days of the upright: and their inheritance shall be for ever . . . For such as be blessed of him shall inherit the earth . . . The righteous shall inherit the land, and dwell therein for ever . . . Wait on the Lord, and keep his way, and he shall exalt thee to inherit the land: when the wicked are cut off, thou shalt see it (Psalms 37:7, 9, 11, 18, 22, 29, 34).

Psalm 68 also refers to the land as an inheritance:

Thou, O God, didst send a plentiful rain, whereby thou didst confirm thine inheritance, when it was weary. Thy congregation hath dwelt therein: thou, O God, hast prepared of thy goodness for the poor (Psalms 68:9-10).

David's Song of Thanksgiving refers to Canaan as an inheritance:

Be ye mindful always of his covenant . . . which He made with Abraham . . . saying, unto thee will I give the land of Canaan, the lot of your inheritance (1 Chronicles 16:15-18).

Psalm 69 refers to inheriting Zion:

For God will save Zion, and will build the cities of Judah: that they may dwell there, and have it in possession. The seed also of his servants shall inherit it: and they that love his name shall dwell therein (Psalms 69:35-36).

Psalm 25 refers to inheriting the earth:

What man is he that feareth the Lord? ...His soul shall dwell at ease; and his seed shall inherit the earth (Psalms 25:12-13).

Psalms 16 and 61 refer to the believer's inheritance more generally:

The Lord is the portion of mine inheritance and of my cup: thou maintainest my lot. The lines have fallen unto me in pleasant places; yea, I have a goodly heritage (Psalms 16:5-6).

For thou, O God, hast heard my vows; thou hast given me the heritage of those that fear thy name (Psalms 61:5).

Psalm 28 refers to the people of God as God's inheritance:

Save thy people, and bless thine inheritance (Psalms 28:9).

11

David's Praise
of the Father

Without directly referring to God as a father, many of David's songs praise God for attributes described as characteristic of His role as father elsewhere in the Bible.

One of those fatherly characteristics is His instructing and leading. In the Twenty-Third Psalm, David praises God for leading him:

He restoreth my soul: he leadeth me in the paths of righteousness for his name's sake (Psalms 23:3).

In other psalms, David calls out to God for leading:

Lead me, O Lord, in thy righteousness because of mine enemies; make thy way straight before my face (Psalms 5:8).

For thy name's sake lead me, and guide me (Psalms 31:3).

Lead me in the way everlasting (Psalms 139:24).

David also calls out to God for teaching and praises God for enlightenment:

Teach me thy way, O Lord; I will walk in thy truth (Psalms 86:11).

For thou art my lamp, O Lord: and the Lord will lighten my darkness (2 Samuel 22:29).

In some psalms, David sings of both leading and teaching:

Shew me thy ways, O Lord; teach me thy paths. Lead me in thy truth, and teach me: for thou art the God of my salvation; on thee do I wait all the day . . . Good and upright is the Lord: therefore will he teach sinners in the way . . . What man is he that feareth the Lord? him shall he teach in the way that he shall choose (Psalms 25:4-5, 8, 12).

Teach me thy way, O Lord, and lead me in a plain path (Psalms 27:11).

I will instruct thee and teach thee in the way which thou shalt go (Psalms 32:8).

Cause me to know the way wherein I should walk; for I lift up my soul unto thee . . . Teach me to do thy will; for thou art my God (Psalms 143:8, 10).

While a human father instructs and leads, David attributes to Jehovah understanding and authority that far exceed those of a human father. David asks God to show him a path or a way. He speaks specifically of a "way everlasting," and of being led in truth and righteousness. David sees Jehovah not merely as a human father but as his God and Father. On the other hand, he sees Jehovah not merely as an abstract god but as his God, who relates to him as a father relates to a son.

David understands that God not only instructs and shows him the way but also supports him and gives him the necessary provisions to follow His leading, as fathers support and provide for their children.

In the Twenty-Third Psalm, David praises God for comforting him:

He maketh me to lie down in green pastures: he leadeth me beside the still waters . . . Yea, though I walk through the valley of the shadow of death, I will fear no evil: for thou art with me; thy rod and thy staff they comfort me (Psalms 23:2, 4).

David also praises God for helping him and upholding him.

Behold, God is mine helper: the Lord is with them that uphold my soul (Psalms 54:4).

Because thou hast been my help, therefore in the shadow of thy wings will I rejoice. My soul followeth hard after thee: thy right hand upholdeth me (Psalms 63:7-8).

The Lord upholdeth all that fall, and raiseth up all those that be bowed down (Psalms 145:14).

God does not mete out provisions meagerly; they are continuous and bountiful:

I will sing unto the Lord, because He hath dealt bountifully with me (Psalms 13:6).

Thou anointest my head with oil; my cup runneth over (Psalms 23:5).

Oh how great is thy goodness, which thou hast laid up for them that fear thee (Psalms 31:19).

Blessed be the Lord, who daily loadeth us with benefits (Psalms 68:19).

Although God sustains every living thing, David repeatedly says that God specially provides for His family. David speaks of God's provisions for His people, the children of Israel:

I laid me down and slept; I awakened; for the Lord sustained me . . . thy blessing is upon thy people (Psalms 3:5, 8).

He made known his ways unto Moses, his acts unto the children of Israel . . . Like as a father pitieth his children, so the Lord pitieth them that fear Him (Psalms 103:7, 13).

Our help is in the name of the Lord, who made heaven and earth (Psalms 124:8).

David praises God for His provisions for the faithful who fear Him:

The Lord preserveth the faithful (Psalms 31:23).

O fear the Lord, ye his saints: for there is no want to them that fear Him. The young lions do lack, and suffer hunger: but they that seek the Lord shall not want any good thing (Psalms 34:9-10).

Cast thy burden upon the Lord, and he shall sustain thee: he shall never suffer the righteous to be moved (Psalms 55:22).

David praises God for His provisions for those who commit to Him and serve Him in His house:

[T]he children of men put their trust under the shadow of thy wings. They shall be abundantly satisfied with the fatness of thy house (Psalms 36:7-8).

Delight thyself also in the Lord; and he shall give thee the desires of thine heart. Commit thy way unto the Lord; trust also in him; and he shall bring it to pass (Psalms 37:4-5).

[G]ive thy strength unto thy servant . . . thou, Lord, hast holpen me, and comforted me (Psalms 86:16-17).

God's support surpasses anything any human can provide. But as with guidance, He does not act remotely as an unapproachable Being. God familiarly supports us, as a father provides for his children.

A fatherly characteristic that David both pleads for and praises God for is His compassion, His lovingkindness:

How excellent is thy lovingkindness, O God! . . . O continue thy lovingkindness unto them that know thee (Psalms 36:7, 10).

Cause me to hear thy lovingkindness in the morning; for in thee do I trust (Psalms 143:8).

God's lovingkindness includes a multitude of tender mercies:

Have mercy upon me, O God, according to thy lovingkindness: according unto the multitude of thy tender mercies blot out my transgressions (Psalms 51:1).

Hear me, O Lord; for thy lovingkindness is good: turn unto me according to the multitude of thy tender mercies (Psalms 69:16).

Lovingkindness is an eternal attribute of God:

Remember, O Lord, thy tender mercies and thy lovingkindnesses; for they have been ever of old (Psalms 25:6).

God's loving-kindness is naturally evident to us, as well as revealed to us through David's psalms:

[T]hy lovingkindness is before mine eyes: and I have walked in thy truth (Psalms 26:3).

I have not concealed thy lovingkindness and thy truth from the great congregation. Withhold not thou thy tender mercies from me, O Lord: let thy lovingkindness and thy truth continually preserve me (Psalms 40:10-11).

We owe God praise for His loving-kindness:

I will worship toward thy holy temple, and praise thy name for thy lovingkindness and for thy truth (Psalms 138:2).

God's lovingkindness is marvelous:

Shew thy marvelous lovingkindness (Psalms 17:7).

Blessed be the Lord: for he hath shewed me his marvelous kindness in a strong city (Psalms 31:21).

God's loving-kindness is better than life:

Because thy lovingkindness is better than life, my lips shall praise thee (Psalm 63:3).

God is full of compassion:

But thou, O Lord, art a God full of compassion, and gracious, longsuffering, and plenteous in mercy and truth (Psalms 86:15).

The Lord is gracious, and full of compassion; slow to anger, and of great mercy (Psalms 145:8).

God bestows His lovingkindness on us like a crown:

Bless the Lord, O my soul . . . Who crowneth thee with loving-kindness and tender mercies (Psalms 103:2-4).

The Hebrew word translated as "lovingkindness" in some verses in the King James Version is also translated as "mercy" in others. In most of those verses, David speaks of God's forgiveness, deliverance, or salvation. In that context, God's lovingkindness stands out as mercy.

In Chronicles, David speaks of God's mercy in a general way:

O give thanks unto the Lord; for He is good; for His mercy endureth for ever. And say ye, Save us, O God of our salvation (1 Chronicles 16:34-35).

David praises God in Psalm 86 for the mercy that he has personally received from God:

For great is thy mercy toward me: and thou hast delivered my soul from the lowest hell (Psalms 86:13).

Sometimes, David praises God for mercy that he expects to receive in the future:

But I have trusted in thy mercy; my heart shall rejoice in thy salvation (Psalms 13:5).

Surely goodness and mercy shall follow me all the days of my life (Psalms 23:6).

He shall send from heaven, and save me from the reproach of him that would swallow me up. Selah. God shall send forth his mercy and his truth (Psalms 57:3).

[T]hy mercy, O Lord, endureth forever (Psalms 138:8).

Sometimes, David calls out to the Lord for mercy:

Return, O Lord, deliver my soul: oh save me for thy mercies' sake (Psalms 6:4).

Hear, O Lord, and have mercy upon me: Lord, be thou my helper (Psalms 30:10).

O God, in the multitude of thy mercy hear me, in the truth of thy salvation (Psalms 69:13).

[B]ecause thy mercy is good, deliver thou me (Psalms 109:21).

Help me, O Lord my God: O save me according to thy mercy (Psalms 109:26).

In the Twenty-Fifth Psalm, David both praises God's mercy and pleads for it:

All the paths of the Lord are mercy and truth unto such as keep his covenant and his testimonies. For thy name's sake, O Lord, pardon mine iniquity; for it is great (Psalms 25:10-11).

God shows vast and eternal mercy to those who fear Him:

For as the heaven is high above the earth, so great is his mercy toward them that fear him. As far as the east is from the west, so far hath he removed our transgressions from us (Psalms 103:11-12).

But the mercy of the Lord is from everlasting to everlasting upon them that fear him (Psalms 103:17).

God shows mercy to those who serve Him:

Also unto thee, O Lord, belongeth mercy: for thou renderest to every man according to his work (Psalms 62:12).

And of thy mercy cut off mine enemies, and destroy all them that afflict my soul: for I am thy servant (Psalms 143:12).

God shows mercy to those who call upon Him:

For thou, Lord, art . . . plenteous in mercy unto all them that call upon thee (Psalms 86:5).

God's mercy is praiseworthy:

I will be glad and rejoice in thy mercy (Psalms 31:7).

I will sing aloud of thy mercy in the morning: for thou hast been my defense and refuge in the day of my trouble. Unto thee, O my strength, will I sing (Psalms 59:16-17).

I will sing of mercy and judgment: unto thee, O Lord, will I sing (Psalms 101:1).

God's mercy is abundant:

But as for me, I will come into thy house in the multitude of thy mercy (Psalms 5:7).

For thy mercy is great unto the heavens, and thy truth unto the clouds (Psalms 57:10).

For thou, Lord, art . . . plenteous in mercy (Psalms 86:5).

The Lord is merciful and gracious, slow to anger, and plenteous in mercy. He will not always chide: neither will he keep his anger for ever (Psalms 103:8-9).

For thy mercy is great above the heavens: and thy truth reacheth unto the clouds (Psalms 108:4).

[T]hou shalt deal bountifully with me (Psalms 142:7).

God's mercy is forever:

His mercy endureth for ever (1 Chronicles 16:34).

But I am like a green olive tree in the house of God: I trust in the mercy of God for ever and ever (Psalms 52:8).

But the mercy of the Lord is from everlasting to everlasting (Psalms 103:17).

[T]hy mercy, O Lord, endureth for ever (Psalms 138:8).

David shows us attributes of a good father that are also attributes of God: instructing and leading, support, compassion, and mercy. Reading and rereading those pleas and praises helps us understand our relationship with God as His children, members of His house.

12

DAVID AND DELIVERANCE

Delivering His children is an attribute of God as our Father. God is our Redeemer and Deliverer who saves us, as Abraham rescued Lot when he was carried away from Sodom, and as David rescued the women and children in his house when they were carried away from Ziklag. David repeatedly sings of that attribute of God.

Some pleas for deliverance are broad:

Preserve me, O God: for in thee do I put my trust (Psalms 16:1).

Hear the right, O Lord, attend unto my cry, give ear unto my prayer (Psalms 17:1).

Save, Lord: let the king hear us when we call (Psalms 20:9).

Be merciful unto me, O God (Psalms 56:1; 57:1).

Preserve my soul; for I am holy (Psalms 86:2).

Many times, David calls out to God for rescue from his enemies:

Keep me as the apple of the eye, hide me under the shadow of thy wings, from the wicked that oppress me, from my deadly enemies, who compass me about (Psalms 17:8-9).

Plead my cause, O Lord, with them that strive with me: fight against them that fight against me (Psalms 35:1).

Deliver me from mine enemies, O my God (Psalms 59:1).

Save with thy right hand, and hear me . . . For he it is that shall tread down our enemies (Psalms 60:5, 12).

Hear my voice, O God, in my prayer: preserve my life from fear of the enemy (Psalms 64:1).

Because thy mercy is good, deliver thou me . . . Help me, O Lord my God: O save me according to thy mercy (Psalms 109:21, 26).

[D]eliver me out of great waters, from the hand of strange children (Psalms 144:7).

In some pleas for deliverance, David sounds near despair:

Lord, how are they increased that trouble me! Many are they that rise up against me. Many there be which say of my soul, there is no help for him in God (Psalms 3:1-2).

Arise, O Lord, in thine anger, lift up thyself because of the rage of mine enemies: and awake for me to the judgment that thou hast commanded (Psalms 7:6).

How long wilt thou forget me, O Lord? For ever? How long wilt thou hide thy face from me? (Psalm 13:1)

My God, my God, why hast thou forsaken me? Why art thou so far from helping me, and from the words of my roaring? (Psalms 22:1)

Hide not thy face far from me . . . Leave me not, neither forsake me, O God of my salvation (Psalms 27:9).

Lord, how long wilt thou look on? Rescue my soul from their destructions, my darling from the lions (Psalms 35:17).

Forsake me not, O Lord: O my God, be not far from me. Make haste to help me, O Lord my salvation (Psalms 38:21-22).

I will say unto God my rock, Why hast thou forgotten me? (Psalms 42:9)

Awake, why sleepest thou, O Lord? Arise, cast us not off for ever . . . Arise for our help, and redeem us for thy mercies' sake (Psalms 44:23, 26).

O God, thou hast cast us off, thou hast scattered us, thou hast been displeased; O turn thyself to us again (Psalms 60:1).

[H]ide not thyself from my supplication. Attend unto me, and hear me (Psalms 55:1-2).

And hide not thy face from thy servant; for I am in trouble: hear me speedily. Draw nigh unto my soul, and redeem it: deliver me because of mine enemies (Psalms 69:17-18).

Make haste, O God, to deliver me (Psalms 70:1).

[M]ake haste unto me (Psalms 141:1).

One time, David began by asking how long but then re-assured himself:

How long shall mine enemy be exalted over me? Consider and hear me, O Lord my God . . . But I have trusted in thy mercy; my heart shall rejoice in thy salvation (Psalms 13:2-3, 5).

In some of his prayers for deliverance, David recalls earlier times when the Lord delivered him from his enemies:

Save me, O my God: For thou hast smitten all mine enemies upon the cheek bone; thou hast broken the teeth of the ungodly. Salvation belongeth unto the Lord (Psalms 3:7-8).

The Lord is my light and my salvation; whom shall I fear? . . . When the wicked . . . came upon me to eat up my flesh . . . they stumbled and fell (Psalms 27:1-2).

He hath delivered me out of all trouble (Psalms 54:7).

He hath delivered my soul in peace from the battle that was against me (Psalms 55:18).

O God the Lord, the strength of my salvation, thou hast covered my head in the day of battle (Psalms 140:7).

In addition to asking for deliverance from his enemies, David asks God for spiritual salvation:

Cleanse thou me from secret faults. Keep back thy servant also from presumptuous sins; let them not have dominion over me: then shall I be upright, and I shall be innocent from the great transgression. Let the words of my mouth, and the meditation of my heart, be acceptable in thy sight, O Lord, my strength, and my redeemer (Psalms 19:12-14).

But as for me, I will walk in mine integrity: redeem me, and be merciful unto me (Psalms 26:11).

[B]e not silent to me: lest, if thou be silent to me, I become like them that go down into the pit . . . Draw me not away with the wicked, and with the workers of iniquity (Psalms 28:1, 3).

O Lord, rebuke me not in thy wrath: neither chasten me in thy hot displeasure . . . Make haste to help me, O Lord my salvation (Psalms 38:1, 22).

Sometimes, while pleading for deliverance, he acknowledges his innumerable sins and anguishes over them:

I said, I will confess my transgressions unto the Lord; and thou forgavest the iniquity of my sin . . . Thou art my hiding place; thou shalt preserve me from trouble; thou shalt compass me about with songs of deliverance (Psalms 32:5, 7).

I will declare mine iniquity; I will be sorry for my sin . . . Make haste to help me, O Lord my salvation (Psalms 38:18, 22).

[M]ine iniquities have taken hold upon me, so that I am not able

to look up; they are more than the hairs of mine head: therefore my heart faileth me. Be pleased, O Lord, to deliver me (Psalms 40:12-13).

David recognizes that he is not only in danger from his enemies but is also in spiritual danger:

> *Save me, O God; for the waters are come in unto my soul. I sink in deep mire, where there is no standing . . . O God, thou knowest my foolishness; and my sins are not hid from thee . . . O God, in the multitude of thy mercy hear me, in the truth of thy salvation. Deliver me out of the mire, and let me not sink: let me be delivered from them that hate me, and out of the deep waters. Let not the waterflood overflow me, neither let the deep swallow me up, and let not the pit shut her mouth upon me . . . let thy salvation, O God, set me up on high* (Psalms 69:1-2, 5, 13-15, 29).

> *O thou my God, save thy servant that trusteth in thee . . . For thou, Lord, art good, and ready to forgive; and plenteous in mercy unto all them that call upon thee . . . For great is thy mercy toward me: and thou hast delivered my soul from the lowest hell* (Psalms 86:2, 5, 13).

David acknowledges that he cannot face God's judgment based on his own righteousness:

> *And enter not into judgment with thy servant: for in thy sight shall no man living be justified* (Psalms 143:2).

He can only depend on God's forgiving all his sins:

> *[T]hou art the God of my salvation; on thee do I wait all the day . . . Look upon mine affliction and pain; and forgive all my sins* (Psalms 25:5, 18).

God grants that forgiveness not because David deserves it but only for God's mercies' sake:

> *O Lord, rebuke me not in thine anger, neither chasten me in thy*

*hot displeasure. Have mercy upon me, O Lord; for I am weak .
. . Return, O Lord, deliver my soul: oh save me for thy mercies'
sake* (Psalms 6:1-2, 4).

*Into thine hand I commit my spirit; thou hast redeemed me, O
Lord God of truth . . . My strength faileth because of mine iniquity . . . deliver me from the hand of mine enemies, and from
them that persecute me. Make thy face to shine upon thy servant:
save me for thy mercies' sake* (Psalms 31:5, 10, 15-16).

*Have mercy upon me, O God, according to thy lovingkindness:
according unto the multitude of thy tender mercies blot out my
transgressions. Wash me thoroughly from mine iniquity, and
cleanse me from my sin* (Psalms 51:1-2).

Sometimes, David asks for the deliverance of all of Israel:

Redeem Israel, O God, out of all his troubles (Psalms 25:22).

Save thy people, and bless thine inheritance (Psalms 28:9).

David receives deliverance and praises God for it. At times,
he speaks not only of his own deliverance but also of God's
delivering all His children from their enemies:

*But the salvation of the righteous is of the Lord: he is their
strength in the time of trouble. And the Lord shall help them,
and deliver them: he shall deliver them from the wicked, and
save them, because they trust in him* (Psalms 37:39-40).

*He that is our God is the God of salvation; and unto God the
Lord belong the issues from death* (Psalms 68:20).

*Be thou exalted, O God, above the heavens: and thy glory above
all the earth; that thy beloved may be delivered: save with thy
right hand, and answer me* (Psalms 108:5-6).

*And say ye, Save us, O God of our salvation, and gather us to-
gether, and deliver us from the heathen, that we may give thanks*

to thy holy name, and glory in thy praise (1 Chronicles 16:35).

At other times David praises God for delivering David from his personal enemies:

The Lord is my rock, and my fortress, and my deliverer . . . He delivered me from my strong enemy, and from them which hated me: for they were too strong for me. They prevented me in the day of my calamity: but the Lord was my stay . . . [H]e delivered me, because he delighted in me (Psalms 18:2, 17-19. See also 2 Samuel 22:2-3, 18-20).

Thou art my hiding place; thou shalt preserve me from trouble (Psalm 32:7).

Mine enemies would daily swallow me up . . . [T]hou hast delivered my soul from death (Psalms 56:2, 13).

[F]or my soul trusteth in thee: yea, in the shadow of thy wings will I make my refuge, until these calamities be overpast . . . He shall send from heaven, and save me from the reproach of him that would swallow me up (Psalms 57:1, 3).

Truly my soul waiteth upon God: from him cometh my salvation . . . My soul, wait thou only upon God; for my expectation is from him. He only is my rock and my salvation: he is my defense; I shall not be moved. In God is my salvation and my glory: the rock of my strength, and my refuge, is in God (Psalms 62:1, 5-7).

Though I walk in the midst of trouble, thou wilt revive me: thou shalt stretch forth thine hand against the wrath of mine enemies, and thy right hand shall save me (Psalms 138:7).

Blessed be the Lord my strength . . . my high tower, and my deliverer (Psalms 144:1-2).

In addition to praising God for deliverance from enemies, David praises God for spiritual deliverance:

[A]s for our transgressions, thou shalt purge them away (Psalms 65:3).

Bless the Lord, O my soul . . . Who redeemeth thy life from destruction . . . As far as the east is from the west, so far hath he removed our transgressions from us (Psalms 103:2-4, 12).

I will extol thee, my God, O King . . . The Lord is gracious, and full of compassion; slow to anger, and of great mercy (Psalms 145:1, 8).

Psalm 34 praises God both as the deliverer from enemies and the deliverer from condemnation:

I sought the Lord, and he heard me, and delivered me from all my fears . . . The Lord is nigh unto them that are of a broken heart; and saveth such as be of a contrite spirit. Many are the afflictions of the righteous: but the Lord delivereth him out of them all . . . The Lord redeemeth the soul of his servants: and none of them that trust in him shall be desolate (Psalms 34:4, 18-19, 22).

As much as a human father devotes himself to protecting his children from harm, God's deliverance far exceeds human protection. God's mercy is from everlasting to everlasting. It provides atonement for our vast iniquities. Even though no one is righteous in His eyes, God does not let the pit shut its mouth on us but delivers our souls from the depths of Sheol. Overwhelming as that fact is, however, we can comprehend it because it is in the manner of Abraham's deliverance of Lot and David's rescue at Ziklag.

13

THE SYNOPTIC GOSPELS ON SONSHIP

We can learn about God as a Father by observing His relationship with His Son, Jesus. We can find an example of perfect behavior as a son by studying Jesus' response to His Father.

JESUS AS THE SON OF GOD, ACCORDING TO MATTHEW

At the end of the Gospel of Matthew, Jesus directed His disciples to make disciples of all nations, teaching them to observe Jesus' commandments. He baptized them "in the name of the Father, and of the Son, and of the Holy Ghost" (Matthew 28:19-20). That reference to the Trinity and the Father-Son relationship in the Trinity shows Jesus' recognition of His role as Son to God the Father and God's role as Father. Jesus referred to those roles in several meaningful contexts throughout the Gospel of Matthew.

As depicted in Matthew, the adult life of Jesus begins and ends with challenges to Jesus to do certain things "if You are the Son of God." After Jesus' baptism, Satan tempted Jesus by twice challenging Him to prove He was God's Son. "If thou be the Son of God," he said, "command that these stones be made bread" (Matthew 4:3). When Jesus refused, he took Jesus to the pinnacle of the temple and said, "If thou be the Son of God, cast thyself down." Jesus again refused, telling him, "It is written . . . thou shalt not tempt the Lord thy God" (Matthew 4:6-7). At Jesus' crucifixion, passersby challenged Him, "If thou be the Son of God, come down from the cross" (Matthew 27:40).

Satan must have known that Jesus was, indeed, the Son of God, unlike the people watching Jesus die. The demons that possessed the two men in the country of the Gergesenes knew. They said to Jesus, "What have we to do with thee, Jesus, thou Son of God? Art thou come hither to torment us before the time?" (Matthew 8:29) Therefore, Satan also knew and rather than disputing that Jesus was the Son of God, he was attempting to lure Jesus into sin.

In contrast, the spectators at the crucifixion were certain that Jesus was not the Son of God. The mob that chose Barabbas over Jesus told Pilate, "His blood be on us and on our children" (Matthew 27:25). They were sure that it was not innocent blood. The people passing by the crucifixion were of the same frame of mind, as is shown by their "wagging their heads" as they spoke (Matthew 27:39).

Regardless of what the challengers intended, the challenge "If You are the Son of God" brackets Matthew's history of Jesus' adult life and emphasizes the pertinence of the relationship of Jesus with God to our relationship with God.

Jesus was also the son of Mary, but he downplayed His human relationships compared to His role in the house of God. Matthew reported the following exchange while Jesus was teaching:

Then one said unto him, Behold, thy mother and thy brethren stand without, desiring to speak with thee. But he answered and said unto him that told him, Who is my mother? And who are my brethren? And he stretched forth his hand toward his disciples, and said, Behold my mother and my brethren! For whosoever shall do the will of my Father which is in heaven, the same is my brother, and sister, and mother (Matthew 12:47-50).

Jesus recognized his kin in the family of God. Throughout the Sermon on the Mount, He spoke to the crowd of God as their Father.

He encouraged them to display good works to "glorify your Father which is in heaven" (Matthew 5:16). He directed them to love their enemies "that ye may be the children of your Father which is in heaven" (Matthew 5:45). He exhorted them to be perfect, "even as your Father which is in heaven is perfect" (Matthew 5:48). He instructed them to do charitable deeds in secret, to pray in secret, and fast in secret, "and thy Father which seeth in secret shall reward thee openly" (Matthew 6:4, 6, 18).

As to prayer, He reassured them that "your Father knoweth what things ye have need of, before ye ask Him." He gave them the Lord's Prayer and told them to begin their prayer by addressing God as "our Father" (Matthew 6:8-9). Having told them to pray to God to "forgive us our debts, as we forgive our debtors," He promised them that if they forgave men their trespasses, "your heavenly Father will also forgive you" (Matthew 6:14).

He advised them not to worry about their lives because "the fowls of the air . . . sow not, neither do they reap . . . yet your heavenly Father feedeth them," and "your heavenly Father knoweth that ye have need of all these things" (Matthew 6:26, 32). He also advised them to ask God to provide, by comparing God's fatherly behavior to their own: "If ye, then, being evil, know how to give good gifts unto your children, how much more shall your Father which is in heaven give good things to them that ask him?" (Matthew 7:11)

After references to "your Father," when Jesus spoke of final judgment and entrance into the kingdom of heaven as a process of selection, He spoke of "My Father." He said, "Not every one that saith unto me, Lord, Lord, shall enter into the kingdom of heaven; but he that doeth the will of my Father which is in heaven. Many will say to me in that day, 'Lord, Lord . . . And then I will profess unto them, I never knew you: depart from me, ye that work iniquity" (Matthew 7:21-23).

Jesus made the same distinction when He sent out His twelve disciples to preach to the lost sheep of the house of Israel. At that time, too, Jesus shifted from speaking of "your Father" to speaking of "my Father." First, Jesus reassured His disciples by reminding them of their relationship with their Father. He counseled them not to fear those who kill the body but cannot kill the soul. He reminded them of the commonness of sparrows and added, "one of them shall not fall on the ground without your Father." Then, after commenting that the disciples were "of more value than many sparrows," he spoke of eternal judgment. Jesus said, "Whosoever therefore shall confess me before men, him will I confess also before my Father which is in heaven. But whosoever shall deny me before men, him will I also deny before my Father which is in heaven" (Matthew 10:29-33).

Shortly before His crucifixion, He spoke of the day He would come with all the angels and sit on the throne of His glory. Jesus said He would say to those on His right hand, "Come, ye blessed of my Father, inherit the kingdom prepared for you from the foundation of the world." Then He would say to those on the left hand, "Depart from me, ye cursed, into the everlasting fire, prepared for the devil and his angels" (Matthew 25:34-41).[11]

Jesus referred to God as His Father when He spoke of the authority granted to Him by God and the authority retained by God. Jesus deferred to His Father's authority without challenge, resentment, or qualification. (See Matthew 11:27, 16:27, 20:20-23, 24:30, 36; 25:31, 34; 26:29, 53; 28:18.) Jesus submitted completely to the will of His Father. Even on the awful matter of the crucifixion, Jesus prayed that the cup might pass from Him "if it be possible," and only "as thou wilt." Matthew reported that "he ... fell on his face, and prayed, saying, O my Father, if it be possible, let this cup pass from me; nevertheless, not as I will, but as thou wilt" (Matthew 26:39).

Jesus referred to God as His Father at times when describing distinctly fatherly behavior by God.

He spoke of God's providing for His children when He told His disciples, "If two of you shall agree on earth as touching any thing that they shall ask, it shall be done for them of my Father which is in heaven" (Matthew 18:19).

Jesus said that ultimate security comes from His Father. Responding to His disciples about a complaint from the Pharisees, He said, "Every plant, which my heavenly Father hath not planted, shall be rooted up" (Matthew 15:13).

Jesus spoke of God's disciplining his children. He told them a story of a king who forgave the debt of a servant who, in turn, did not ignore what someone owed to him. When the king learned what the servant had done, he delivered the ser-

---

[11] Judgment and grace are discussed in the last chapter.

vant to the torturers until he paid his debt. Jesus said, "So likewise shall my heavenly Father do also unto you, if ye from your hearts forgive not every one his brother their trespasses" (Matthew 18:23-35).

In addition to providing for his children and disciplining them, a father instructs his children. Jesus spoke of His Father's revealing truths to His children. When Peter declared Jesus to be "the Christ, the Son of the living God," Jesus told him he was blessed because that had been revealed to him by "My Father which is in heaven" (Matthew 16:16-17). Jesus thanked His Father for revealing truths as He determined (Matthew 11:25-26).

Jesus' thanking His Father is significant both for displaying God in the fatherly role of revealing truths to His children and for showing Jesus behaving as a good Son, thanking His Father for His actions.

Jesus made an effort to spend time with His Father, for example, by going up on a mountain by Himself to pray (Matthew 14:23).

God spoke twice of the relationship. After John baptized Jesus, God spoke from heaven, saying, "This is my beloved Son, in whom I am well pleased" (Matthew 3:17). During the transfiguration, God spoke from a bright cloud, saying, "This is My beloved Son, in whom I am well pleased. Hear ye him!" (Matthew 17:5)

JESUS AS THE SON OF GOD, ACCORDING TO MARK

The Gospel of Mark repeats many references to the Father-Son relationship between God and Jesus that are in

Matthew. Included are the two incidents of God's stating His love for His Son at the baptism and the transfiguration that are in Matthew (Mark 1:11; 9:7). Mark 5:7 describes the cry of despair by demons that is in Matthew. Mark 8:38 recounts the prediction by Jesus of His coming again in the glory of His Father that is also in Matthew.

In reporting on Jesus' agony in Gethsemane, Matthew reported, "And he went a little farther, and fell on his face, and prayed, saying, O my Father, if it be possible, let this cup pass from me; nevertheless, not as I will, but as thou wilt" (Matthew 26:39). Mark reported the same facts with slightly different wording: "And he went forward a little, and fell on the ground, and prayed that, if it were possible, the hour might pass from him. And he said, Abba, Father, all things are possible unto thee; take away this cup from me: nevertheless not what I will, but what thou wilt" (Mark 14:35-36). Mark indicated that Jesus said *Father* twice, once in Aramaic, *Abba*.

Some assert that *abba* is a sentimental term best translated as "daddy." The context here suggests a sense of obedience.

G. Campbell Morgan observed about Jesus' prayer to His Father in Gethsemane that:

> *There was cooperation with God in that very surrender of the will. This is not the picture of a vacillating soul, but that of the soul . . . yielded to God.[12]*

Paul's use of the word, once in writing to the Romans and once in writing to the Galatians, supports the sense of obedience. He referred to believers as adopted children of God, using the word *abba* to address God as Father:

---

[12] G. Campbell Morgan, *The Gospel According to Mark*, Revell, 1927, page 299.

For as many as are led by the Spirit of God, they are the sons of God. For ye have not received the spirit of bondage again to fear; but ye have received the Spirit of adoption, whereby we cry, Abba, Father. The Spirit itself beareth witness with our spirit, that we are the children of God: and if children, then heirs; heirs of God, and joint-heirs with Christ (Romans 8:14-17).

But when the fullness of the time was come, God sent forth his Son, made of a woman, made under the law, to redeem them that were under the law, that we might receive the adoption of sons. And because ye are sons, God hath sent forth the Spirit of his Son into your hearts, crying, Abba, Father. Wherefore, thou art no more a servant, but a son; and if a son, then an heir of God through Christ (Galatians 4:4-7).

Adoption suggests a connotation of obedience in using the term *abba*. In adoption, the new parent acquires an obligation to the child of support, and the new child accepts a reciprocal responsibility to the parent of obedience.

In "Arise, My Soul, Arise," Charles Wesley sang the praise of Abba, Father:

My God is reconciled; His pard'ning voice I hear;
He owns me for His child, I can no longer fear;
with confidence, I now draw nigh, with confidence I now draw
nigh, and "Father, Abba, Father!" cry.

G. Campbell Morgan quotes Bernard, in his Bampton Lectures, as describing Mark as "the Gospel of action, rapid, vigorous, vivid."[13] Consistent with that description, Mark tells about significant events of Jesus' life with little embellishment. In that style of quickly stating the happenings, Mark presents additional statements about Jesus' relationship as Son of God.

---

[13] G. Campbell Morgan, *op. cit*, page 9.

First, Mark stated it by opening the book with the words, "The beginning of the gospel of Jesus Christ, the Son of God" (Mark 1:1).

Jesus said it when questioned by the high priest. The high priest asked, "Art thou the Christ, the Son of the Blessed?" Jesus answered, "I am: and ye shall see the Son of man sitting on the right hand of power, and coming in the clouds of heaven" (Mark 14:61-62).

Finally, a gentile witness at the crucifixion, a centurion, expressed it when he said, "Truly this man was the Son of God" (Mark 15:39).

JESUS AS THE SON OF GOD, ACCORDING TO LUKE

The Gospel of Luke repeats many references to Jesus as the Son of God that are reported in Matthew and Mark.

Luke recounts God's expressing His love for His Son at the baptism of Jesus. However, unlike Matthew and Mark, Luke uses the second person, with God addressing Jesus rather than onlookers: "a voice came from heaven which said, 'Thou art My beloved Son; in thee I am well pleased'" (Luke 3:22). It also tells of God's expressing His love for Jesus at the transfiguration, but this time in the third person, addressed to onlookers, as in Matthew and Mark: "There came a voice out of the cloud, saying, This is My beloved Son: hear him" (Luke 9:35).

Like Matthew, Luke narrates Satan's challenges to Jesus to prove He was the Son of God, which Satan began with the words, "If thou be the Son of God" (Luke 4:3, 9). Like Matthew and Mark, Luke reports on demons' calling Jesus "Son of God" (Luke 4:41; 8:28).

Along with Mark, Luke tells of Jesus' looking ahead to His coming again in glory, which is not only His but also His Father's glory. Luke adds that it is the angels' glory too (Luke 9:26).

Luke reports Jesus' reference to God's revealing truths as He determined, although Matthew described Jesus as thanking His Father for that, and Luke portrays Jesus as praising His Father for that (Luke 10:21). Like Matthew, in Luke 10:22, Jesus says, "All things are delivered to me of my Father: and no man knoweth who the Son is, but the Father" (Luke 10:22).

Just as in Matthew and Mark, in Luke 22:42, Jesus asks His Father to remove the cup from Him if it is His Father's will. However, the passage adds that God, showing fatherly support and compassion, sent an angel from heaven to strengthen His Son (Luke 22:43).

Luke reports, along with Mark, Jesus' telling the elders that He is the Son of God (Luke 22:70-71).

Luke provides more detail on God's role as Father in the conception of Jesus. Matthew merely says, "When as his mother Mary was espoused to Joseph, before they came together she was found with child of the Holy Ghost" (Matthew 1:18).

Luke tells of the visit of the angel Gabriel to Mary, "a virgin espoused to a man whose name was Joseph, of the house of David" (Luke 1:27). Gabriel told Mary that she would "conceive in [her] womb . . . a son," who "shall be called the Son of the Highest" (Luke 1:31-32). When Mary asked, "How shall this be, seeing I know not a man?" Gabriel elaborated on the manner of that conception as follows: "The Holy Ghost shall come upon thee, and the power of the Highest shall overshadow thee: therefore also that holy thing which shall be born of thee shall be called the Son of God" (Luke 1:34-35).

Luke provides more information than Matthew and Mark on Jesus' spending time with His Father.

Luke reports that when Jesus was twelve years old, He went to Jerusalem with Joseph and Mary for the Feast of the Passover and stayed behind in Jerusalem instead of returning home with Joseph and Mary. For three days, He sat in the temple, listening to the teachers and asking them questions, astonishing onlookers with his understanding. He explained that He "must be about my Father's business" (Luke 2:41-49).

Luke portrays Jesus as often involved in prayer. In Galilee, "He withdrew himself into the wilderness, and prayed" (Luke 5:16). Before choosing the twelve disciples, "He went out into a mountain to pray, and continued all night in prayer to God" (Luke 6:12). After feeding the five thousand, "He was alone praying" when the disciples joined Him and discussed who He was (Luke 9:18). The transfiguration occurred "as He prayed" (Luke 9:29). He taught the disciples the Lord's Prayer at their request after He completed praying (Luke 11:1). And finally, He prayed in agony to His Father in Gethsemane to remove the cup from Him (Luke 22:41-44).

Luke reports that Jesus spoke to His Father twice while on the cross. First, He prayed, "Father, forgive them; for they know not what they do" (Luke 23:34). Before He died, He said, "Father, into thy hands I commend my Spirit" (Luke 23:46).

These acts of Jesus show us, in a way His words cannot, that His identity as Son of God is not merely symbolic (although it has symbolic importance). It is an actual relationship in which Jesus spends time with His Father, and His Father responds to Jesus' needs.

Shortly before His crucifixion, Jesus told His disciples, "I appoint unto you a kingdom, as my Father hath appointed unto me; that ye may eat and drink at my table in my kingdom, and sit on thrones judging the twelve tribes of Israel" (Luke 22:29-30). Jesus passed on to other children of God the inheritance from God. After His crucifixion, He commented on the passing of the inheritance through His death on the cross, saying:

> *Thus it is written, and thus it behoved Christ to suffer, and to rise from the dead the third day: and that repentance and remission of sins should be preached in his name among all nations, beginning at Jerusalem . . . And, behold, I send the promise of my Father upon you* (Luke 24:46-49).

Jesus' kinship with the children of God, like the one with His Father, is a vital relationship. It is a bond in which Jesus transfers the benefits and obligations, and the children of God accept and act on them.

14

JOHN ON SONSHIP

The Gospel of John richly describes Jesus' relationship with God as His Father. Understanding John's reporting of that relationship is central to our understanding of God the Father and Jesus as His Son, and of our roles as children of God and members of His house.

The Gospel of John includes Jesus' dramatic statement, "In my Father's house are many mansions," and the promise that "I go to prepare a place for you" (John 14:2). He explains, "If a man love me, he will keep my words: and my Father will love him, and we will come unto him, and make our abode with him" (John 14:23).

John quotes Jesus' using family terms in speaking to Mary Magdalene following Jesus' resurrection, saying, "Go to my brethren, and say unto them, I ascend unto my Father, and your Father; and to My God and your God" (John 20:17).

John calls Jesus "the only begotten of the Father" (John 1:14) and God's "only begotten Son" (John 1:18; 3:16), who "is in the bosom of the Father" (John 1:18). In addition to the many times Jesus called God His Father, Jesus called Himself the Son of God. When Jews sought to kill Him because He "said also that God was His Father, making himself equal with God" (John 5:18), He reiterated in detail His near identity with His Father:

Verily, verily, I say unto you, the Son can do nothing of himself, but what he seeth the Father do: for what things soever he doeth these also doeth the Son likewise. For the Father loveth the Son, and sheweth him all things that himself doeth; and he will shew him greater works than these, that ye may marvel. For as the Father raiseth up the dead, and quickeneth them; even so the Son quickeneth whom he will. For the Father judgeth no man, but hath committed all judgment unto the Son: that all men should honour the Son, even as they honour the Father. He that honoureth not the Son honoureth not the Father which hath sent him (John 5:19-23).

Later, people gathered rocks to stone Him for blaspheming by calling Himself the Son of God. He told them to "believe the works [I did]: that ye may know, and believe, that the Father is in me, and I in him" (John 10:38).

When Pilate told the chief priests and officers that he found no fault in Jesus, they answered, "By our law he ought to die, because he made himself the Son of God" (John 19:7). When Pilate asked Jesus for a response, Jesus merely said, "He that delivered me unto thee hath the greater sin" (John 19:11).

John the Baptist proclaimed that Jesus was the Son of God, saying, "And I saw, and bare record that this is the Son of God" (John 1:34). When John the Baptist explained to his disciples that Jesus "must increase, but I must decrease," (John 3:30), he told them that:

The Father loveth the Son, and hath given all things into his hand. He that believeth on the Son hath everlasting life: and he that believeth not the Son shall not see life; but the wrath of God abideth on him (John 3:35-36).

Nathanael said to Jesus, "Thou art the Son of God; thou art the King of Israel" (John 1: 49). Simon Peter said to Him,

"Thou art that Christ, the Son of the living God" (John 6:69). John, in his Gospel, states that "These are written, that ye might believe that Jesus is the Christ, the Son of God; and that believing ye might have life through his name" (John 20:31).

The Gospel of John provides a detailed view of Jesus' relationship with God in the description of His prayer in chapter 17. In direct communication with God, Jesus addressed God as "Father" six times (John 17:1, 5, 11, 21, 24, 25) and referred to Himself as "thy Son" (John 17:1). Jesus described God's relationship with Him in distinctly parental terms. It is an intimate, yet hierarchical, relationship, with God standing in authority over Jesus. God exercised that authority by sending Jesus on a mission.

The relationship is a loving relationship. Jesus said, "Thou hast loved me," (John 17:23, 26), and He said, "Thou lovest me before the foundation of the world" (John 17:24).

Jesus also expressed that God loved His other children, whom Jesus referred to as "the men which thou gavest me out of the world" (John 17:6). Jesus said, "Thou . . . hast loved them, as thou hast loved Me" (John 17:23). Jesus described His efforts to build that family relationship, saying, "I have declared unto them thy name, and will declare it: that the love wherewith thou hast loved me may be in them, and I in them" (John 17:26). Having done the work the Father sent Him to do, He prayed to the Father to make His children one, as the Father and the Son are one (John 17:11, 21-23).

The relationship of Jesus to God is close. Although Jesus said to His Father, "The world hath not known thee," He declared, "I have known thee" (John 17:25). Jesus expressed unity with His Father. He said, "Thou, Father, art in me, and I in thee" (John 17:21). He also said, "We are one" (John 17:22).

Despite Jesus' expressions of intimacy, Jesus acknowledged that God had authority over Him. Jesus said three times that His glory came from God (John 17:1, 5, 24). God delegated some power, but not complete discretion, to Jesus. Jesus began His prayer by stating (referring to Himself in the third person as "thy Son"), "Thou hast given him power over all flesh, that he should give eternal life to as many as thou hast given him" (John 17:2). God gave Jesus authority to give eternal life to those whom God gave to Jesus. Jesus repeatedly referred to the people God gave to Him, not just in verse 2 and in verse 6 (quoted above, in the discussion of love in the relationship), but also in verses 9, 11, 12, and 24.

Jesus emphasized that God sent Jesus to work for Him. Jesus said six times that God sent Him (John 17:3, 8, 18, 21, 23, 25). Jesus declared that He has done the work that God sent Him to do, saying, "I have glorified thee on the earth: I have finished the work which thou gavest me to do" (John 17:4).

He elaborated on the work He had done. He declared God's name to the men God gave to Him (John 17:6, 26). He gave those men the words God gave to Him (John 17:8, 14). He kept them in God's name (John 17:12). He sanctified Himself so that they also may be sanctified (John 17:19). He sent them into the world, as God sent Him into the world (John 17:18). In sending them forth, He further delegated authority to the children of God in His role as firstborn among many brethren.

Throughout his Gospel, John imparts the theme of intimacy between God and Jesus that Jesus expressed in His prayer.

Jesus said, "Therefore doth my Father love me, because I lay down my life, that I might take it again" (John 10:17). He said to His disciples, "As the Father hath loved Me, so have I loved you" (John 15:9). He invited them to "continue ye in my love" and to "abide in my love" (John 15:9-10). The love extended in both directions in the father-son relationship. Jesus stated His intention "that the world may know that I love the Father" (John 14:31).

As He had done in His prayer, He spoke of God's love for His children. Jesus said, "He that loveth me shall be loved of my Father . . . If a man love me, he will keep my words; and my Father will love him" (John 14:21, 23). To His disciples, He said, "the Father himself loveth you, because ye have loved me, and have believed that I came out from God" (John 16:27).

Like Jesus' saying in His prayer, "We are one," the Gospel of John uses the image of unity throughout in describing the relationship between Jesus and His Father. John describes Jesus as "in the bosom of the Father" (John 1:18). He reports that Jesus said, "The Father is in me, and I in him" (John 10:38), and "I and my Father are one" (John 10:30). Jesus told His disciples, "He that hateth me hateth my Father also" (John 15:23).

To the Pharisees who accused Jesus of lying and challenged Him, saying, "Where is thy Father," He said, "If ye had known me, ye should have known my Father also" (John 8:19). Similarly, when Thomas said, "Lord, we know not whither thou goest; and how can we know the way?" Jesus replied, "I am the way . . . If ye had known me, ye should have known my Father also: and from henceforth ye know him and have seen him." Phillip said, "Lord, shew us the Father, and it sufficeth us." Jesus responded, "He that hath seen me hath seen the Father; and how sayest thou then, Shew us the Father?

Believest thou not that I am in the Father, and the Father in me? . . . the Father that dwelleth in me, he doeth the works. Believe me that I am in the Father, and the Father in me: or else believe me for the very works' sake" (John 14:5-11).

In speaking of that unity, Jesus did not mean to say He was God the Father. His many references to His Father as being distinct from Him, such as references to His Father's sending Him and statements such as, "My Father is greater than I" (John 14:28), and especially His prayer to His Father, show that. He used that image of unity to express the closeness of their relationship. He also used it to describe the intimacy of His relationship with His Father's other children, saying, "Because I live, ye shall live also. At that day ye shall know that I am in my Father, and ye in me, and I in you" (John 14:19-20).

Jesus spoke of the knowledge of each other that He and His Father have (John 8:55; 10:15). Jesus said His Father had not left Him alone but was with Him (John 8:16, 29; 16:32).

As Jesus claimed authority from His Father in His prayer, He spoke of that authority elsewhere in the Gospel of John, as did John the Baptist.

John the Baptist told his disciples, "The Father . . . hath given all things into his hand" (John 3:35). Jesus rose from the Passover feast "knowing that the Father had given all things into his hands" (John 13:3). Jesus told His disciples, "All things that the Father hath are mine" (John 16:15).

Jesus said, "The Father judgeth no man, but hath committed all judgment unto the Son" (John 5:22). Referring to those who follow Him, Jesus said His Father had given them to Him (John 6:37-40; 10:29). Jesus said that His Father testified of Him (John 5:37), set His seal on Him (John 6:27), and bore witness of Him (John 8:18). He told those who sought to kill Him for saying that God was His father, "I am come in my Father's name" (John 5:43). To those who asked Him if He was the Christ, He said, "The works that I do in my Father's name, they bear witness of me" (John 10:25).

Jesus' emphasis in His prayer on His Father's sending Him mirrors His emphasis on God's sending Him throughout the Gospel of John. Eleven times, in addition to the six times in His prayer, Jesus said that God sent Him (John 5:30, 36-37; 6:44, 57; 8:16, 18; 10:36; 12:49; 14:24; 20:21). Each time, Jesus referred to God as Father.

In addition to using the word *sent*, He twice said that God, as Father, gave Him to the world. He said, "For God so loved the world, that he gave his only begotten Son, that whosoever believeth in him should not perish, but have everlasting life" (John 3:16). Referring to Himself, He said, "My Father giveth you the true bread from heaven" (John 6:32).

Jesus was sent to do His Father's work. He said, "My Father worketh hitherto, and I work" (John 5:17). He referred to "the works which the Father hath given me to finish" (John 5:36). Jesus' direction in how to do that work came from His Father. Jesus said, "the Son can do nothing of himself, but what He seeth the Father do: for what things soever he doeth, these also doeth the Son likewise. For the Father . . . sheweth him all things that himself doeth" (John 5:19-20).

Jesus' guidance in what to say also came from His Father. He said, "the Father which sent me, he gave me a commandment, what I should say, and what I should speak" (John 12:49). He also said, "I speak that which I have seen with my Father" (John 8:38).

Jesus fulfilled His Father's directions. He said, "I seek not mine own will, but the will of the Father which hath sent me" (John 5:30). "I honour my Father," He said, "and keep his saying" (John 8:49, 55). Jesus told His disciples, "As the Father gave me commandment, even so I do" (John 14:31). Then He described Himself as the true vine, His disciples as the branches, and His Father as the vinedresser. Jesus said, "I have kept my Father's commandments," and instructed them to keep His commandments (John 15:1-10).

Jesus followed God's direction as to His speech. He said, "As my Father hath taught me, I speak these things" (John 8:28). Similarly, Jesus said, "Whatsoever I speak therefore, even as the Father said unto me, so I speak" (John 12:50). He told His disciples, "The words that I speak unto you I speak not of myself" (John14:10). Furthermore, Jesus said, "The word which ye hear is not mine, but the Father's which sent me" (John 14:24). He also told them, "All things that I have heard of my Father I have made known unto you" (John 15:15).

Jesus followed His Father's direction as to His actions. He said, "Many good works have I shewed you from my Father" (John 10:32). He did it without fail. He said, "I do always those things that please him" (John 8:29). The ultimate command He received from His Father, which He fulfilled, was to lay down His life (John 10:17-18).

Having completed His mission, He returned to His Father (John 13:1; 14:2, 12; 16:10, 16, 28; 20:17).

15

OVERVIEW OF SONSHIP

Jesus had a close relationship of mutual love with God in heaven. God, as Father, stood in authority over Jesus. God exercised that authority in sending His Son on a mission to bring other children into the family. God effected a physical birth of Jesus into this world through the Holy Spirit's coming upon Mary, a virgin.

At the beginning of His ministry on Earth, Satan challenged Jesus to prove He is the Son of God. At the end, passersby challenged Jesus to come down from the cross if He was the Son of God. Nonetheless, Jesus repeatedly called Himself the Son of God and called God His Father. God twice called Jesus His beloved Son. Mark's Gospel begins with Mark's statement that Jesus is the Son of God. John's Gospel begins with John's calling Jesus God's only begotten Son. It ends by saying that John wrote it so the reader might believe that Jesus is God's Son and have life in His name. John the Baptist, Nathanael, Simon Peter, unclean spirits, and a Roman centurion at the crucifixion all called Jesus the Son of God.

Jesus spent much time with His Father in prayer and spoke to His Father while on the cross. God gave Jesus the authority He needed to complete His mission and gave Jesus loving support. Jesus, in return, loved His Father, deferred entirely to His Father's authority, and thanked His Father for His actions.

Jesus loved those whom God sent Him to save and served as a means for God to love them. Jesus told them of God and that God was their Father too. He told them of God's love for them, His providing for them, His disciplining them, and His revelation to them.

Jesus said He always did those things that pleased His Father, and God declared He was well pleased with Jesus. Jesus said what His Father directed Him to say and did what His Father directed Him to do. He returned to be with His Father in a house with many mansions to prepare a place for God's other children. He promised to "make our home" with them.

Can we draw lessons from Jesus' relationship with His Father to help us relate to God the Father? It would be easy to shy away from claiming any similarities with Jesus. We may be children of God, but Jesus was the only begotten Son of God. He was "In the beginning . . . with God, and . . . was God" (John 1:1). How can we presume to say we are like Him at all?

Nonetheless, as the author of Hebrews said, "Both he that sanctifieth and they who are sanctified are all of one: for which cause he is not ashamed to call them brethren" (Hebrews 2:11). Jesus called upon us to identify with Him, saying, "He that abideth in me, and I in him, the same bringeth forth much fruit" (John 15:5).

Jesus maintained a close relationship with His Father by communicating with Him through prayer. That is not only something we can do; it is something Jesus directed us to do. He gave us a model in the Lord's Prayer. He instructed us to "pray to thy Father" (Matthew 6:6).

Jesus acknowledged that His Father was the source of all that He had and asked His Father for support in time of need. Likewise, He told us of our Father's providing for us: "Take no thought, saying, What shall we eat? or What shall we drink? or, Wherewithal shall we be clothed?" (Matthew 6:31). He told us to ask for more, saying, "If ye, then, being evil, know how to give good gifts unto your children, how much more shall your Father which is in heaven give good things to them that ask him?" (Matthew 7:11) He taught us in the Lord's Prayer to ask not only for our daily bread but also for forgiveness, protection from temptation, and deliverance from the evil one (Matthew 6:11-13).

Charles Wesley expressed that filial request to the Father to protect him from temptation in his hymn, "I Want a Principle Within":

> From Thee that I no more may stray,
> No more Thy goodness grieve,
> Grant me the filial awe, I pray,
> The tender conscience give.
> Quick as the apple of an eye,
> O God, my conscience make!
> Awake my soul when sin is nigh,
> And keep it still awake.

In the same way that Jesus prayed for those His Father had given Him out of the world (John 17:6-26), we should pray for our brothers and sisters in God's house. Jesus prayed "that they all may be one" (John 17:21). We can pursue that unity by praying for each other. We can also pursue it by praying together, as Jesus directed in Matthew 18:19-20.

Just as Jesus thanked His Father for revealing truths as He determined (Matthew 11:25-26), we should thank our Father for what He does for us and for being who He is.

Jesus submitted to His Father's authority. He prayed to His

Father in anguish in the Garden of Gethsemane that the cup would pass from Him but prayed for that only "if it be possible" and prayed "not as I will, but as thou wilt" (Matthew 26:39). Jesus was obedient to His Father's will, declaring to His Father, "I have finished the work which thou gavest me to do" (John 17:4). Obedience is the duty of all children, including the children of God. Jesus said, "Whosoever shall do the will of my Father which is in heaven, the same is my brother, and sister, and mother" (Matthew 12:50). He also said, "If ye keep my commandments, ye shall abide in my love, even as I have kept my Father's commandments, and abide in his love" (John 15:10). He sent us forth into the world as the Father sent Him into the world (John 17:18).

In submitting to our Father's authority, we must not only do as He commands but also accept His discipline when we fail and change to conform to His will. We should remember our Father gives us directions and discipline out of love, and as Jesus did, love Him in return.

16

RUSSELL AND DESPOTS

To understand who God is, it helps to examine who God is not. From time to time, a prominent thinker will argue that God does not exist by describing their image of God and attacking it. Typically those images are contrary to the picture of God as Father provided by the Bible. The biblical image disproves their arguments, and our reviewing those arguments enhances our appreciation of how the Bible describes God.

Bertrand Russell built his argument against God on an image of God as a despot. Understanding God as Father shows that whatever complaint one may have about God and our relationship with God, God is no despot.

In explaining why he was not a Christian, Bertrand Russell conceded, "I do not pretend to be able to prove that there is no God."[14] However, that did not discourage him from arguing that there is no God. One approach he took was to set up various arguments that he characterized as attempting to prove the existence of God—the First Cause Argument, the Natural-Law Argument, the Argument from Design, the Moral Argument, and the Argument for the Remedying of Injustice—and presuming to knock them down.

---

[14] Bertrand Russell, *Why I Am Not a Christian*, Touchstone, 1957, page 50.

Another approach was to give his analysis of how the idea of God originated and dismiss its basis as unsound. He saw God as a despot, modeled on despotic rulers of the ancient world. He started with, "Religion is based, I think, primarily and mainly upon fear."[15] The response to that fear, in his view, was, "If the world is controlled by God, and God can be moved by prayer, we acquire a share in omnipotence."[16] He elaborated by describing his view of the virtuous life:

> In the orthodox Christian conception, the good life is the virtuous life, and virtue consists in obedience to the will of God, and the will of God is revealed to each individual through the voice of conscience. This whole conception is that of men subject to an alien despotism.[17]

That repeated what he had said earlier in the book: "The whole conception of God is a conception derived from the ancient Oriental despotisms."[18] He suggested, "We, who belong to great democracies, should find a more appropriate morality in free Athens than in despotic Imperial Rome."[19] He described the progression from primitive religion to his ideal of rejecting the "slavishness" of worshiping force, which is to say, God:

> The savage, like ourselves, feels the oppression of his impotence before the powers of nature; but having in himself nothing that he respects more than power, he is willing to prostrate himself before his gods, without inquiring whether they are worthy of his worship . . . But gradually, as morality

---

[15] *Id.*, page 22.
[16] *Id.*, page 53.
[17] *Id.*, page 74.
[18] Id., page 23.
[19] *Id.*, page 73.

grows bolder, the claim of the ideal world begins to be felt
... Some, though they feel the demands of the ideal, will
still consciously reject them, still urging that naked power
is worthy of worship. Such is the attitude inculcated in
God's answer to Job out of the whirlwind ... But others,
not content with an answer so repugnant to the moral sense,
will adopt the position that ... in some hidden manner, the
world of fact is really harmonious with the world of ideals.
Thus man created God, all-powerful and all-good, the mys-
tic unity of what is and what should be. But the world of
fact, after all, is not good; and, in submitting our judgment
to it, there is an element of slavishness from which our
thoughts must be purged ... Shall we worship force, or shall
we worship goodness? Shall our God exist and be evil, or
shall he be recognized as the creation of our own con-
science?[20]

He expanded on the question, "Shall our God exist and be
evil," insisting that there is no good in the concept of God:

It is true that Christianity and all previous optimisms have
represented the world as eternally ruled by a beneficent
Providence, and thus metaphysically good. But this has
been, at bottom, only a device by which to prove the future
excellence of the world—to prove, for example, that good
men would be happy after death.[21]

Understanding God as a father would lead to an entirely
different conclusion. Russell had to ignore the biblical image
of God as a father to put forth his despotism argument.
Indeed, despotic fathers do exist. The ideal, however, is that
while a father asserts authority and punishes rebellion, he loves

[20] *Id.,* pages 107-109.
[21] *Id.,* pages 98-99.

his children and is gracious to them. A flaw in Russell's argument reveals a flaw in his characterization of God as an evil despot: What evil despot "can be moved by prayer"? Unlike a cruel despot, a loving father is moved by his children's pleas, as is God.

17

FREUDIANS AND FANTASY

Sigmund Freud observed the importance of the role of God as Father but recognized only the label and not the substance, as described in the Bible, of that role. In *Totem and Taboo*, he said, "If psycho-analysis deserves any attention, then—without prejudice to any other sources or meanings of the concept of God, upon which psycho-analysis can throw no light—the paternal element in the concept must be a most important one."[22] However, characterizing God as Father did not help him understand God better without reference to the Bible. On the contrary, Freud concluded that characterizing God as Father proves that God does not exist.

Freud asserted that man has imagined the existence of God as the fulfillment of a wish for an omnipotent father to protect us against the dangerous forces of nature and humankind. He made the argument this way in *The Future of an Illusion*:

> As we already know, the terrifying impression of helplessness in childhood aroused the need for protection—for protection through love—which was provided by the father; and the recognition that this helplessness lasts throughout life made it necessary to cling to the existence of a father, but this time a more powerful one. Thus the benevolent rule of

[22] *The Standard Edition of the Complete Psychological Works of Sigmund Freud*, Volume XIII, The Hogarth Press, 1961 edition, page 147.

a divine Providence allays our fear of the dangers of life ... Answers to the riddles that tempt the curiosity of man ... are developed in conformity with the underlying assumptions of this system. It is an enormous relief to the individual psyche if the conflicts of its childhood arising from the father-complex—conflicts which it has never wholly overcome—are removed from it and brought to a solution which is universally accepted.[23]

Freud asserted that the usefulness of an omnipotent father proves the concept's falsity. In *The Future of an Illusion*, he claimed, "To assess the truth-value of religious doctrines does not lie within the scope of the present inquiry." However, he immediately turned from that disclaimer and said:

We know approximately at what periods and by what kind of men religious doctrines were created. If in addition we discover the motives which led to this, our attitude to the problem of religion will undergo a marked displacement. We shall tell ourselves that it would be very nice if there were a God ... but it is a very striking fact that all this is exactly as we are bound to wish it to be.[24]

In *Civilization and Its Discontents*, he said:

The derivation of religious needs from the infant's helplessness and the longing for the father aroused by it seems to me to be incontrovertible, especially since the feeling is not simply prolonged from childhood days, but is permanently sustained by fear of the superior power of Fate ... The origin of the religious attitude can be traced back in clear outlines as far as the feeling of infantile helplessness.[25]

---

[23] *The Standard Edition of the Complete Psychological Works of Sigmund Freud*, Volume XXI, The Hogarth Press, 1961 edition, page 30.
[24] *Id.*, page 33.
[25] *Id.*, page 72.

To argue that a god who meets our needs as a father meets the needs of his children cannot exist because those needs are deeply felt is illogical. Freud himself stated, "Illusions need not necessarily be false—that is to say, unrealizable or in contradiction to reality. For instance, a middle-class girl may have the illusion that a prince will come and marry her. This is possible; and a few such cases have occurred."[26] But Freud could not restrain himself from jumping from the "very striking fact" of the wish-fulfillment to the conclusion that "the origin of the religious attitude" is in "the feeling of infantile helplessness."

Freud could arrive at that conclusion only by starting from the presupposition that no god exists. If a god created us, we should not be surprised if that god meets our needs or if we desire that god to meet our needs. Furthermore, we should not be surprised if that god expressed His relationships with us as being like our relationships with each other so that we can better understand our relationships with Him.

Erich Fromm agreed with Freud that religion is a "collective fantasy."[27] He also agreed that some religious belief, what he called "authoritarian religion," derives from man's wish for parental protection. He arrived at that conclusion by expanding on Freud's concept of the Oedipus complex:

> Freud states that the Oedipus complex is the core of every neurosis. His assumption is that the child is bound to the parent of the opposite sex and that mental illness results if the child does not overcome this infantile fixation . . . As is

[26] *Id.*, page 31.

[27] Erich Fromm, *The Dogma of Christ and Other Essays on Religion, Psychoanalysis and Culture*, Holt, Rinehart and Winston, 1963 edition, page 20.

often the case, however, the full significance of Freud's discovery can be recognized only if we translate it from the sphere of sex into that of interpersonal relations. The essence of incest is not the sexual craving for members of the same family. This craving, in so far as it is to be found, is only one expression of the much more profound and fundamental desire to remain a child attached to those protecting figures of whom the mother is the earliest and most influential . . . As long as man is related by these primary ties to mother, father, family, he feels protected and safe.[28]

However, Fromm disagreed with Freud's claim that "the unreality of the theistic concept is demonstrated by exposing it as an illusion based on man's wishes."[29] While Fromm agreed that authoritarian religion is an illusion, he disagreed with Freud's belief that the proof that it is an illusion lies in the fact that it fulfills wishes. Fromm asserted, "The criterion of validity does not lie in the psychological analysis of motivation but in the examination of evidence for or against a hypothesis within the logical framework of the hypothesis."[30] That is, our wanting something to exist does not make it imaginary. Proving that it does not exist requires evidence.

Nonetheless, the only evidence Fromm offered against the hypothesis of a parental god was his belief that relating to a god as a child to a parent is a harmful relationship. It is harmful, he believed, because it prevents the child's development:

By remaining a child man not only avoids the fundamental anxiety necessarily connected with the full awareness of

---

[28] Erich Fromm, *Psychoanalysis and Religion*, Yale University Press, 1950 edition, pages 79-80.
[29] *Id.*, page 12.
[30] *Id.*, page 12, n. 1.

oneself as a separate entity, he also enjoys the satisfactions of protection, warmth, and of unquestioned belonging which he once enjoyed as a child; but he pays a high price. He fails to become a full human being, to develop his powers of reason and of love; he remains dependent and retains a feeling of insecurity which becomes manifest at any moment when these primary ties are threatened. All his mental and emotional activities are geared to the authority of his primary group; hence his beliefs and insights are not his own. He can feel affection but it is animal affection, the warmth of the stable, and not human love which has freedom and separateness as its condition ... He is incapable of relating himself closely to the "stranger," that is, to another human being as such.[31]

It is accurate to say of a child of God that "his beliefs and insights are not his own." Isaiah quotes God as saying, "Come now, and let us reason together" (Isaiah 1:18). God makes clear, however, that the only acceptable reasoning is reasoning on God's terms. God explains what He means by *reason together*: "If ye be willing and obedient, ye shall eat the good of the land: but if ye refuse and rebel, ye shall be devoured with the sword" (Isaiah 1:19-20).

That would be harmful if God were an Oedipally-induced illusion. But if a god existed who knew all that could be known, such a god clearly would be superior to humankind in reasoning, meriting our respect. He would have useful knowledge and deserve our attention. If that god were good, that god's imparting any knowledge to humankind, and that god's insisting that humankind accept and live by that knowledge, would be beneficial for humankind. The Bible reveals that such a God

---

[31] *Id.*, page 80.

exists and that He does that for humankind, as a father does for his children.

Although Fromm was correct in asserting that a child of God is not free to form his own beliefs, he was wrong in asserting that a child of God cannot love beyond feeling "animal affection." Consider the love Moses displayed in offering himself as an atonement for the sins of other human beings (foreshadowing Jesus' dying for humankind). When the Israelites made a golden calf, Moses pleaded with God, "Oh, this people have sinned a great sin, and have made them gods of gold. Yet now, if thou wilt forgive their sin—;and if not, blot me, I pray thee, out of thy book which thou hast written" (Exodus 32:31-32). On an individual level, consider the tender love expressed in David's eulogy upon learning of Jonathan's death in battle: "I am distressed for thee, my brother Jonathan: very pleasant hast thou been unto me: thy love to me was wonderful, passing the love of women" (2 Samuel 1:26).

God paternalistically tells us how to think, and we resent the authoritarianism of that. But God, as our loving Father, is the source of our love. God gives us the capacity to love. John says, "Love is of God" (1 John 4:7). Having enabled us to love, God shows us how to love by His example. John further tells us, "We love him, because he first loved us" (1 John 4:19). Jesus said, "This is my commandment, that ye love one another, as I have loved you" (John 15:12).

Fromm said that a child of God "fails to become a full human being," but on the contrary, the life of a child of God is a life of continuous growth and fulfillment. Paul said, "We beseech you, brethren, and exhort you by the Lord Jesus, that . . . ye would abound more and more" (1 Thessalonians 4:1). He spoke eloquently of strengthening and fulfilling the inner man, through love, in the family of God:

*For this cause I bow my knees unto the Father of our Lord Jesus
Christ, of whom the whole family in heaven and earth is named,
that He would grant you, according to the riches of His glory, to
be strengthened with might by his Spirit in the inner man; that
Christ may dwell in your hearts by faith; that ye, being rooted
and grounded in love, may be able to comprehend with all saints
what is the breadth, and length, and depth, and height; and to
know the love of Christ, which passeth knowledge, that ye might
be filled with all the fullness of God* (Ephesians 3:14-19).

Fromm spoke of "humanistic religion," which he defined
as follows: "Inasmuch as humanistic religions are theistic, God
is a symbol of *man's own powers*, which he tries to realize in his
life, and is not a symbol of force and domination, having *power
over man*."[32] Fromm approvingly asserted that "early
Christianity is humanistic and not authoritarian," arguing that
to be "evident from the spirit and text of all Jesus' teachings."[33]
However, the examination of Jesus in His role as Son of God
shows how the God that Jesus revealed is a consistently paternal God, authoritarian, in addition to loving, contrary to
Fromm's assertion.

In "The Dogma of Christ," Fromm used his view of the
parental element of the concept of God to propose that social
conditions created early Christianity and then changed it dra-
matically within the first three centuries. Fromm described the
early Christians as "the poor, uneducated, oppressed masses of
the Jewish people, and later, of other peoples."[34] According to

---

[32] Erich Fromm, *Psychoanalysis and Religion*, page 37.

[33] *Id.*, page 48.

[34] Erich Fromm, *The Dogma of Christ and Other Essays on Religion,
Psychoanalysis and Culture*, Holt, Rinehart and Winston, 1963 edition,
page 41.

Fromm, they expressed their oppression in their religion as follows:

> Conscious hatred was reserved for the authorities, not for the elevated father figure, the divine being himself. But the unconscious hostility to the divine father found expression in the Christ fantasy. They put a man at God's side and made him a co-regent with God the father. This man who became a god, and with whom as humans they could identify, represented their Oedipus wishes; he was a symbol of their unconscious hostility to God the father, for if a man could become God, the latter was deprived of his privileged fatherly position of being unique and unreachable. The belief in the elevation of a man to god was thus the expression of an unconscious wish for the removal of the divine father.[35]

He then described "what transformation Christianity underwent during the first three centuries, and how the new religion contrasted with the old."[36] It was a "transformation of Christianity from the religion of the oppressed to the religion of the rulers and of the masses manipulated by them."[37] That transformation came about because "The social system was stabilized and was regulated from the top, and it was important to make it easier for the individual who stood at the bottom to be content with his situation."[38] Fromm asserted that the social change brought about a new religion:

> The strong, powerful father has become the sheltering and protecting mother ... Under the guise of the fatherly God

[35] *Id.*, page 47.
[36] *Id.*, page 56.
[37] *Id.*, page 60.
[38] *Id.*, page 56.

of the Jews, who in the struggle with the Near Eastern motherly divinities had gained dominance, the divine figure of the Great Mother emerges again, and becomes the dominating figure of medieval Christianity.

The significance the motherly divinity had for Catholic Christianity, from the fourth century on, becomes clear, first, in the role that the Church, as such, begins to play; and second, in the cult of Mary ... The Church mediates salvation, the believers are her children, she is the Great Mother through whom alone men can achieve security and blessedness.

Equally revealing is the revival of the figure of the motherly divinity in the cult of Mary. Mary represents that motherly divinity grown independent by separating itself from the father-god. In her, the motherly qualities, which had always unconsciously been a part of God the father, were now consciously and clearly experienced and symbolically represented.[39]

He concluded:

Catholicism signified the disguised return to the religion of the God Mother who had been defeated by Yahweh. Only Protestantism turned back to the father-god.[40]

Fromm's evidence does not support his argument that humankind invented early Christianity in response to social conditions. His evidence is that people resented control and therefore resented God the Father. However, people resented God's authority and rebelled against Him long before the birth of Christianity. Beginning with Adam and Eve and the tree of

---

[39] *Id.*, page 68.
[40] *Id.*, page 91.

knowledge of good and evil, proceeding through the behavior that brought the judgment of the flood, and including the betrayal of God by Israel as portrayed in Hosea, humankind has openly expressed conscious hostility towards God's authority. Fromm need not try to explain humankind's rebellion against God, nor Jesus' deity, by the oppression of the Jewish masses at the time of Jesus.

Fromm was right to examine the Catholic Church's perception of Mary and to ask why "from a recipient of grace she became a dispenser of grace."[41] However, he concluded that Catholicism constituted a return to the start, in a progression of people creating a maternal god, then replacing her with a paternal god, and then returning to a maternal god due to the paternal god's inadequacies. The true nature of God's paternal character refutes Fromm's conclusions.

Fromm was near the truth in observing that "the motherly qualities . . . had always . . . been a part of God the father," but missed a complete understanding in saying it was unconsciously a part. God's qualities of sheltering and protecting are overt and recognized throughout Scripture.

Understanding the full extent of the parental qualities of God, as described in Scripture, would avoid the mistake of saying that "the Great Mother" is the god "through whom alone men can achieve security and blessedness."

---

[41] *Id.*, page 69.

18

GOULD AND FUNNY SOLUTIONS

Stephen Jay Gould argued that there is no god because a perfect god would have perfect creations, perfect creatures. If he understood God as Father, God as head of the house of God, the authoritative head of the household, and a creative creator who creates as it pleases Him, he would have seen his logic break down.

Gould argued against the creation of animals by a god by pointing to animals' imperfections. He cited the wrist bone that the panda uses as a thumb for grasping bamboo as a useful but imperfect instrument:

> The panda's true thumb is committed to another role, too specialized for a different function to become an opposable, manipulating digit. So the panda must use parts on hand and settle for an enlarged wrist bone and a somewhat clumsy, but quite workable, solution. The sesamoid thumb wins no prize in an engineering derby. It is, to use Michael Ghiselin's phrase, a contraption, not a lovely contrivance.[42]

He argued that such inelegance shows that an omnipotent god could not have created the panda:

---

[42] Stephen Jay Gould, *The Panda's Thumb*, W.W. Norton & Company, New York, N.Y., 1980, page 24.

Our textbooks like to illustrate evolution with examples of optimal design ... But ideal design is a lousy argument for evolution, for it mimics the postulated action of an omnipotent creator. Odd arrangements and funny solutions are the proof of evolution—paths that a sensible God would never tread but that a natural process, constrained by history, follows perforce.[43]

That argument fails to understand God's role as a father. It fails to account for God's authority. In His role as head of the house, God does as He sees fit, not as we see fit. Psalm 115 says, "Our God is in the heavens: he hath done whatsoever he hath pleased" (Psalm 115:3). Psalm 135 says:

Ye that stand in the house of the Lord, in the courts of the house of our God, praise the Lord ... For I know that the Lord is great, and that our Lord is above all gods. Whatsoever the Lord pleased, that did he in heaven, and in earth, in the seas, and all deep places (Psalm 135:2-3, 5-6).

As often happens to rebellious children examining their father's actions, what pleases God can appear to us to be poorly done. God presents those apparently irrational acts to us as reminders of His absolute authority.

Job told God that He had poured Job out as milk and curdled him like cheese (Job 10:10) and asked God, "Wherefore then hast thou brought me forth out of the womb?" (Job 10:18) Then God revealed His power and authority to Job by reminding Job not only of the grand things He had done but also of those things that may seem absurd to us. God began by asking Job, "Where wast thou when I laid the foundations of the earth?" (Job 38:4) But He also reminded Job that His

---

[43] *Id.*, pages 20-21.

creation is not entirely rational from humanity's point of view. He challenged Job with the question:

> *Who hath divided a watercourse for the overflowing of waters ... to cause it to rain on the earth, where no man is; on the wilderness, wherein there is no man ... ?* (Job 38:25-26)

Similarly, God pointed out to Job the foolish, inelegant ostrich:

> *Which leaveth her eggs in the earth, and warmeth them in dust, and forgetteth that the foot may crush them, or that the wild beast may break them. She is hardened against her young ones, as though they were not hers: her labour is in vain without fear; because God hath deprived her of wisdom, neither hath he imparted to her understanding* (Job 39:14-17).

Considering God's entire speech to Job is necessary to understand why God called attention to the ostrich. God expressed to Job God's power and Job's weakness. God reminded Job that God is the Creator of all, and that Job is one of His creatures. God began by saying, "Wilt thou also disannul my judgment? Wilt thou condemn me, that thou mayest be righteous?" (Job 40:8) Job understood. He answered, "I know that thou canst do every thing, and that no thought can be withholden from thee" (Job 42:2).

Gould attempted to annul God's judgment by calling it a "funny solution," but would have done better to have acknowledged that no purpose of God's can be withheld from Him, even if it appears pointless to us.

God did not make the panda inelegant and the ostrich foolish out of neglect or even out of arbitrariness. God did that as an expression of His authority. Gould said that processes like those that produced the panda are "paths that a sensible God would never tread." God's creating the panda and the ostrich, with their quirks, defies those who boast of having sufficient wisdom to determine through their logic what is sensible for God.

Isaiah quoted God as saying, "I am the Lord . . . that turneth wise men backward" (Isaiah 44:24-25). Paul elaborated on those who appear wise in secular terms, saying, "If any man among you seemeth to be wise in this world, let him become a fool, that he may be wise" (1 Corinthians 3:18). Paul explained that "God hath chosen the foolish things of the world to confound the wise . . . that no flesh should glory in his presence" (1 Corinthians 1:27-29).

God created the world and continues to interact with it on His terms, not on Gould's, and not on your terms or mine. To have a proper relationship with God, we must accept Him as Father, exercising authority on His terms, not ours.

19

TWAIN AND FAIRNESS

Mark Twain made the strongest argument against God of all the critics—the problem of evil. Understanding God as Father does not solve the problem, but it helps us understand a world where evil occurs, and people suffer, and it helps us relate to the God who created it.

Twain, in *The Mysterious Stranger*, portrayed a world in which humans suffer continually, substantially, and unjustifiably at the hands of people and the hand of God.

He presented human life as a tragic existence characterized by suffering, which a god who is at best arbitrary and arguably sadistic inflicts on humans. In one incident, a god-like act of creation of tiny people is followed by the "wanton murder" of two of the tiny people by their creator, who is named Satan. The creator stops in mid-sentence to observe a fight between the two, and the narrator describes his reaction as follows:

> Satan reached out his hand and crushed the life out of them with his fingers, threw them away, wiped the red from his fingers, and went on talking where he had left off.[44]

Other tiny people hold a funeral, and further bloodshed ensues. The narrator tells that:

---

[44] Mark Twain, *The Mysterious Stranger and Other Stories*, Signet Classic, page 170.

[T]he small noise of the weeping and praying began to annoy him, then he reached out and took the heavy board seat out of our swing and brought it down and mashed all of those people into the earth just as if they had been flies, and went on talking just the same.[45]

Twain's view of human life echoed that of the Earl of Gloucester in Shakespeare's *King Lear*, who said, "As flies to wanton boys, are we to th' gods, they kill us for their sport."[46]

At the end of the tale, Twain answered the question of how such a god could exist by describing the narrator's realization that no such god exists, and further, that neither the narrator nor the world around him exists. Instead, "It is all a dream—a grotesque and foolish dream."[47]

But knowing God as Father helps us accept that it is accurate and that God is real.

Because Twain presumably believed, contrary to the outcome of his story, that the world exists, he apparently considered that God might exist as well but resented God's allowing suffering. The tale emphasizes the unfairness of the suffering and concludes with a tirade against God, who "mouths justice." Yet Twain himself was ambivalent about whether man is always good, deserving no punishment, or sometimes bad, deserving punishment.

He described most men as good, saying, "In any community, big or little, there is always a fair proportion of people who are not malicious or unkind by nature, and who never do unkind things except when they are overmastered by fear, or

[45] *Id.*, page 171.
[46] *The Yale Shakespeare*, "King Lear," Act IV, Scene 1, line 36.
[47] Mark Twain, *The Mysterious Stranger and Other Stories*, Signet Classic, page 253.

when their self-interest is greatly in danger, or some such matter as that."[48] Again he said, "The vast majority of the race, whether savage or civilized, are secretly kindhearted and shrink from inflicting pain, but in the presence of the aggressive and pitiless minority they don't dare to assert themselves."[49]

However, Twain also described human beings as naturally given to torturing each other, tending to "inflict pain for the pleasure of inflicting it."[50] He characterized the human race as "always lying, always claiming virtues which it hasn't got."[51] As to a man's moral sense, he said, "He is always choosing, and in nine cases out of ten he prefers the wrong."[52] He said, "The first man was a hypocrite and a coward, qualities which have not yet failed in his line."[53]

Although Twain sometimes seemed to sense that perhaps suffering is justified by unruly behavior, he remained angry at God for not fixing it so that no punishment would be necessary. He ranted against "a God who could make good children as easily as bad yet preferred to make bad ones."[54]

He stood at the threshold of understanding when he referred to the children of God, but he did not understand the full nature of God as Father. A father must maintain authority over and discipline his child for his instruction to be effective and for the child to grow. First Kings 1 shows the result of David's failure to discipline Adonijah. Hebrews says, "What

[48] *Id.*, page 202.
[49] *Id.*, page 238.
[50] *Id.*, pages 192-193.
[51] *Id.*, page 192.
[52] *Id.*, page 193.
[53] *Id.*, page 234.
[54] *Id.*, page 253.

son is he whom the father chasteneth not?" (Hebrews 12:7). A father requires repentance from a wayward child and rewards repentance with mercy.

Jesus told a parable of a son who took his part of the inheritance, went away, and squandered it all. He returned to his father, repenting, saying, "Father, I have sinned against heaven, and before thee, and am no more worthy to be called thy son" (Luke 15:18-19). The father celebrated and took the son back as a member of his household.

At the beginning of His ministry, Jesus preached, "Repent ye, and believe the gospel" (Mark 1:15). When the Mark Twains of His day confronted Him with the apparent unfairness of the deaths of worshipers "whose blood Pilate had mingled with their sacrifices," instead of apologizing, Jesus told them, "Except ye repent, ye shall all likewise perish" (Luke 13:1, 3).

Repentance requires not only a confession of one's sin but also recognition that the sin places us in conflict with God, humble acceptance of our guilt and punishment, and resolve to do better. (See Leviticus 26:40-42 and Psalm 51.)

God the Father will respond to such repentance by restoring our relationship with Him (Leviticus 26:42). In His parable of prayer, Jesus said that the tax collector who prayed, "God be merciful to me a sinner," through humbling himself, "went down to his house justified" (Luke 18:13-14). David concludes a psalm of repentance by reassuring himself, "a broken and a contrite heart, O God, thou wilt not despise" (Psalm 51:17). Paul told the Corinthians, "Godly sorrow worketh repentance to salvation" (2 Corinthians 7:10).

Some refuse to repent. The Bible tells us that, even in the Tribulation, when God's judgment is clear to all, men will blaspheme rather than repent (Revelation 16:9, 11). In *The Mysterious*

Stranger, Mark Twain chose to berate God for allowing evil to exist and allowing men to embrace it rather than admit that a man has any personal responsibility for his bad behavior.

Nonetheless, we must not dismiss glibly the problem that Twain addressed. We do not know why God, in His omnipotence, did not eliminate the need for repentance.

Rabbi Harold Kushner concluded that God must not be omnipotent:

> I recognize His limitations. He is limited in what He can do by laws of nature and by the evolution of human nature and human moral freedom. I no longer hold God responsible for illnesses, accidents, and natural disasters, because I realize that I gain little and I lose so much when I blame God for those things. I can worship a God who hates suffering but cannot eliminate it, more easily than I can worship a God who chooses to make children suffer and die, for whatever exalted reason.[55]

Rabbi Kushner's conclusion is unconvincing since it is based on his yearning for actions by God that would make it easier for him to worship God. Also, his conclusion that a good and omnipotent god could not allow suffering is based on the false premise that people are good.

He conceded that there are very few totally unselfish people but asserted that "We often find ourselves asking why ordinary people, nice friendly neighbors, neither extraordinarily good nor extraordinarily bad, should suddenly have to face the agony of pain and tragedy."[56] Even with that concession, he overrated humankind.

---

[55] Harold Kushner, *When Bad Things Happen to Good People*, Schochen Books 1981 edition, page 134.
[56] *Id.*, page 8.

The Bible teaches consistently that no man is good. David said, "There is none that doeth good" (Psalms 14:1 and 53:1). Solomon said, "There is no man that sinneth not" (1 Kings 8:46; 2 Chronicles 6:36). The author of Ecclesiastes, believed to have been Solomon, said, "There is not a just man upon earth, that doeth good, and sinneth not" (Ecclesiastes 7:20). Isaiah said, "All we like sheep have gone astray" (Isaiah 53:6). Jeremiah said, "The heart is deceitful above all things, and desperately wicked" (Jeremiah 17:9). Micah said, "There is none upright among men" (Micah 7:2). Jesus said, "None is good, save one, that is God" (Luke 18:19). First John 1:8 says, "If we say that we have no sin, we deceive ourselves." Paul said, quoting David, "There is none that doeth good, no, not one" (Romans 3:12).

Still, establishing that humankind does not meet God's standards does not answer Mark Twain's question of why "a God who could make good children as easily as bad . . . preferred to make bad ones." Job said to God, "Why hast thou set me as a mark against thee, so that I am a burden to myself? And why dost thou not pardon my transgression, and take away mine iniquity?" (Job 7:20-21) Although his tone was more respectful than Twain's, he asked the same question.

Job's three friends tried to justify suffering as appropriate punishment for sin. Eliphaz, for example, said to Job, "Where were the righteous cut off? . . . they that plow iniquity, and sow wickedness, reap the same" (Job 4:7-8). God dismissed Eliphaz's position, telling Eliphaz, "Ye have not spoken of me the thing that is right" (Job 42:7). However, God gave no explanation in its place. Instead, God responded to Job by declaring His power and glory in Job 38-41. God restored Job but left the question unanswered. His response essentially was that we are not entitled to an answer.

When Job cried out, "Oh . . . that the Almighty would answer me" (Job 31:35), Elihu said, "I will answer thee, that God is greater than man. Why dost thou strive against him? For he giveth not account of any of his matters" (Job 33:12-13).

God responded as Elihu said He would, demanding of Job:

Who is this that darkeneth counsel by words without knowledge?
. . . I will demand of thee, and answer thou me (Job 38:2-3).

God said, in this relationship, the one who will ask the questions is *I,* and the one who will give the answers is *you.* Job responded by saying, "What shall I answer thee? I will lay mine hand upon my mouth" (Job 40:4). God, however, demanded an answer. He said, "I will demand of thee, and declare thou unto me" (Job 40:7). He followed up by asking Job how he could presume to challenge God, saying, "Wilt thou condemn me, that thou mayest be righteous?" (Job 40:8). He spoke again of His glory and Job's weakness. Job answered God that time, acknowledging that he had challenged God through a lack of understanding of God and that he now saw God, and his relationship to God, in a new light:

Therefore have I uttered that I understood not; things too wonderful for me, which I knew not . . . I have heard of thee by the hearing of the ear; but now mine eye seeth thee (Job 42:3, 5).

Job repented, saying, "I . . . repent in dust and ashes" (Job 42:6). That repentance went far beyond confessing specific sins and accepting guilt for them. Job said, "I abhor myself" (Job 42:6). He repudiated himself. He completely humbled himself before God. Our insisting on having the right to an answer from God, as Twain did, is part of our problem with God. We should pray to God, as Job did, but we should not challenge His authority by demanding that He defend His actions. We should not challenge Him even about our suffering.

Twain's error was in presuming to define what a perfect God would be on his terms and dismissing Jehovah for not fitting that definition. Gould did the same thing in *The Panda's Thumb*. God responded to both Twain and Gould in the book of Job by refusing to apologize or explain.

As head of the household, the message is that He expects to be respected and expects His children to accept the relationship He created when He created us. Demanding an explanation dishonors God, and believing we could understand the reason is arrogance. Accepting that is difficult for us all, not just for Twain and Gould, but embracing it is the path to a rich relationship with God as Father.

God allows suffering and does not tell us why. As Father, however, God has lovingly and graciously shared the burden.

At the end of His ministry, Jesus continued to preach repentance, tying it to His death on the cross. Jesus told His disciples that "it behoved Christ to suffer, and to rise from the dead the third day: and that repentance and remission of sins should be preached in his name among all nations, beginning at Jerusalem" (Luke 24:46-47). For the remission of sins, Jesus took the punishment as the Lamb of God, and God gave Jesus up to that. The Gospel of John reports that John the Baptist identified Jesus as the Lamb of God, and it explains: "God so loved the world, that he gave his only begotten Son, that whoever believeth in him should not perish, but have everlasting life" (John 3:16).

We do not know why God made us and our world as He did. We know that as His children, we may not challenge His choices. We also know that, through Jesus, the Trinity experienced human suffering. Most importantly, as our Father, God has provided a solution to the problem of sin: Jesus, the Lamb of God, who has provided everlasting life where "there shall be no more death, neither sorrow, nor crying, neither shall there be any more pain: for the former things are passed away" (Revelation 21:4). Compared to that, "Our light affliction . . . is but for a moment" (2 Corinthians 4:17).

Further, as Timothy Keller explains, the future is "not a future that is just a consolation for the life we never had but a restoration of the life you always wanted." As Jesus said in Matthew 19:28, it is the regeneration, "the renewal of all things."[57]

---

[57] Timothy Keller, *The Reason For God*, Dutton, 2008, pages 32-33.

20

DIFFERENT PATHS TO THE SAME TRUTH

Some say that different religions are merely different paths to the same truth. Various reasons are given for that argument. One reason is to avoid dissension by finding a common ground. Huston Smith advises:

> We must listen first to our own faith, for every heritage is inexhaustible . . . But we must also listen to the faiths of others . . . The community today can be no single tradition; it is the planet. Daily the world grows smaller, leaving understanding the only bridge on which peace can find its home.[58]

One reason is to have the philosophical satisfaction of finding a unified theory of divinity. John Hick proposes "a general theory of religion which is intended to be acceptable to the more global-minded members of all traditions."[59]

Another reason is the fear that, given the inability to prove the validity of any religion, no religion can justifiably claim to be valid if it denies the truth of any other faith. John Hick argues as follows:

---

[58] Huston Smith, *The Religions of Man*, Perennial Library 1965 edition, pages 354-355.
[59] John Hick, *An Interpretation of Religion*, Yale University Press 1989 edition, page 10.

Nor can we reasonably claim that our own form of religious experience, together with that of the tradition of which we are a part, is veridical whilst the others are not. We can of course claim this; and indeed virtually every religious tradition has done so, regarding alternative forms of religion either as false or as confused and inferior versions of itself. But the kind of rational justification set forth in Chapter 13 for treating one's own form of religious experience as a cognitive response – though always a complexly conditioned one—to divine reality must ... apply equally to the religious experience of others.[60]

The levels of inclusiveness vary. Some, like Smith and Hick, assert that all religions are merely ways of attempting to express a single divine reality. Some argue more narrowly that Christianity, Judaism, and Islam—as monotheistic religions—all worship the same god.

The biblical descriptions of the house of God and God as the paternalistic head of that house stand in the way of those assertions. Understanding the God of the Bible as Father distinguishes that God from the god of the Koran. It also reveals a character of that God that prevents us from ignoring Him as a distinct personality in a search for spirituality.

---

[60] *Id.*, page 235.

21

THE GOD OF ISLAM

It is tempting to treat Jehovah and Allah as the same entity. The fact that the Koran speaks of many of the historical figures mentioned in the Bible and many of the events reported in the Bible, encourages that.

The Koran in some ways equates Allah with the God of Abraham, Isaac, and Jacob, retelling stories from the Old Testament and, in doing so, calling God "Allah." It expressly directs Muslims as follows in dealing with Jews:

> Do not argue with the people of the Book …, and say to them: "We believe what has been sent down to us, and we believe what has been sent down to you. Our God and your God is one, and to Him we submit" Sura 29, 46.[61]

However, the description of Allah in the Koran is markedly different from the description of Jehovah in the Old Testament, particularly as to the role of Jehovah as Father. The Koran never describes Allah as a father. Apart from characterizing Allah as lord, the one relationship the Koran describes between Allah and man is that of friend, saying, "God chose Abraham as friend" Sura 4, 125.[62]

---

[61] Al-Qur'an, A Contemporary Translation by Ahmed Ali, Princeton University Press, Princeton, New Jersey, 2001, page 340.
[62] Id., page 90.

149

The image of God's considering Abraham as a friend is consistent with the Bible's description of their relationship. God spoke of that relationship as follows:

> *But thou, Israel art My servant, Jacob whom I have chosen, the seed of Abraham my friend* (Isaiah 41:8).

In the Bible, God had a similar relationship with Moses. Exodus tells us that, "The Lord spake unto Moses face to face, as a man speaketh unto his friend" (Exodus 33:11).

While the Bible goes beyond the relationship of friend to describe God as Father and Head of the House of God, the Koran stops at the image of friend. Although the Koran presents Allah as the God of Israel, it emphasizes repeatedly the difference between the Christian God and Allah, and cites Jehovah's role of Father to make that distinction. It says repeatedly, sometimes vehemently, that Jesus is not the Son of God. The point is summed up in the third sura from the end, which says that Allah is "God the one the most unique …. He has begotten no one, and is begotten of none" Sura 112, 1-3.[63]

The Koran states many more times that Allah has begotten no son.[64] It states that Jesus was only an apostle,[65] only a creature.[66] Allah is too glorious,[67] too exalted,[68] too immaculate,[69]

---

[63] *Id.*, page 559.

[64] See Sura 2, 115-116, id. at page 25, Sura 6, 101-102, id. at page 125, Sura 17,111, id. at page 249, Sura 18, 4-5, id. at page 250, Sura 25, 2, id. at page 306, Sura 39, 4, id. at page 391, Sura 43, 81, id. at page 422.

[65] Sura 3, 49, id. at page 56, Sura 4, 157, id. at page 93, Sura 4, 171, id. at page 95, and Sura 5, 75, id. at page 108.

[66] Sura 43, 59, id. at page 421.

[67] Sura 4, 171, id. at page 95, Sura 23, 91, id. at page 295, and Sura 43, 82, id. at page 422.

[68] Sura 21, 26, id. at page 276.

[69] Sura 19, 35, id. at page 262.

too holy,[70] to have a son. It says Allah is one god alone,[71] and it warns against having two gods.[72] To say that Allah has begotten a son, or to speak of the Trinity, is to say blasphemous,[73] terrible,[74] grievous[75] words of disbelief,[76] which "would cleave the skies asunder, rend the earth, and split the mountains,"[77] warranting severe, painful punishment,[78] even damnation.[79]

The Koran puts the words in the mouth of Jesus in the cradle, quoting the baby Jesus as saying, "I am a servant of God.... He has given me a Book and made me a prophet."[80] It says, when Allah will ask Jesus if He told mankind to worship Him as a deity, Jesus will answer that He did not, having no right to say that.[81]

The Koran not only denies that Jesus is the only begotten Son of God. It also rejects the biblical characterization of believers as sons and daughters of God.[82] The Koran describes believers as inheritors of the earth,[83] but as trustees, not as children.[84]

---

[70] Sura 9, 31, id. at page 165.

[71] The verses saying Allah is one god are too numerous to break out in a list. See, for example, Sura 2, 163, id. at page 30.

[72] Sura 16, 51, id. at page 232, and Sura 17, 22, id. at page 242.

[73] Sura 9, 32, id. at page 165.

[74] Sura 18, 5, id. at page 250.

[75] Sura 19, 89, id. at page 265

[76] Sura 5, 17, id. at page 100, and Sura 5, 73, id. at page 107-108.

[77] Sura 19, 90, id. at page 265.

[78] Sura 5, 73, id. at page 108, and Sura 10, 70, id. at page 184.

[79] Sura 5, 72, id. at page 107, and Sura 9, 30, id. at page 165.

[80] Sura 19, 30, id. at pages 261-262.

[81] Sura 5, 116, id. at page 113.

[82] Sura 5, 18, id. at page 100, and Sura 6, 100, id. at page 124.

[83] Sura 19, 40, id. at page 262.

[84] Sura 6, 165, id. at page 132, and Sura 43, 60, id. at page 421

The Koran states emphatically and consistently that its god is no one's father. No one can believe that Jehovah and Allah are the same if they understand the importance in the Bible of Jehovah's role as father in the Trinity and as father at the head of the House of God, and the importance in the Koran of the principle that Allah is neither father of Jesus nor father of believers.

22

THE GRAND BELIEF

In Herman Melville's *Moby Dick*, the narrator, who calls himself Ishmael, tells the pious Quaker Bildad that the idol-worshiping Queequeg is a member of the First Congregational Church, by which he means:

> The same ancient Catholic Church to which you and I, and Captain Peleg there, and Queequeg here, and all of us, and every mother's son and soul of us belong; the great and ever-lasting First Congregation of this whole worshipping world; we all belong to that; only some of us cherish some queer crotchets noways touching the grand belief; in that we all join hands.[85]

What Melville called "queer crotchets," Huston Smith called "differences in character of local traditions and civilizations," as follows:

> If God is a God of love, it seems most unlikely that he would not have revealed himself to his other children as well. And it seems probable that his revelation would have taken different facets and different forms according to the differences in nature of individual souls and the differences in character of local traditions and civilizations. This is one possible contemporary meaning of Paul's statement about "one spirit, many gifts." One who holds this view will find many things in other

---

[85] Herman Melville, *Moby Dick*, Pocket Books 1999 edition, page 105.

religions that puzzle and disturb, but will see their light as deriving basically from the same source as his own.[86]

In *An Interpretation of Religion,* John Hick attempted to show how all religions could derive their light from the same source by suggesting "a general theory of religion."[87] Because he found "the Divine" and "the Eternal One" to be "perhaps too theistically colored," he suggested "the Real" as being "as good a generic name as we have for that which is affirmed in the varying forms of transcendent religious belief."[88] He proposed that different religions "represent different phenomenal awarenesses of the same noumenal reality and evoke parallel salvific transformations of human life."[89]

According to Hick, the unifying quality of all religions is "a radical turning from ego to the ultimately Real."[90]

He described that process in advaitic Hinduism as follows:

[W]e are in our true nature one with the eternal reality of Brahman. But this ultimate identity is at present obscured by the empirical ego, the self-positing "I" which encases and conceals the inner self. The "I" is part of the samsaric illusion of . . . the world of perpetual change and unfulfillment through which the . . . soul passes in the course of many earthly lives until it attains to liberation . . . When this happens, in the words of a contemporary interpreter of advaitic Hinduism, "The small human individualistic self disappears and the universal atman now takes its place."[91]

---

[86] Smith, *op. cit.,* page 353.
[87] Hick, *op. cit.,* page 10.
[88] *Id.,* page 11.
[89] *Id.,* page 15.
[90] *Id.,* page 43.
[91] *Id.,* page 37.

He described the process of "turning from the ego to the ultimately Real" in Buddhism as follows:

"Buddhist salvation is . . . nothing other than an awakening to reality through the death of the ego." . . . This turning from ego to reality is both illuminated and enabled by the anatta ('no self') doctrine, which D.T. Suzuki translates as "non-ego," "selflessness," and which he says "is the principal conception of Buddhism, both Hinayana and Mahayana."[92]

He acknowledged that Christianity does not call for negating the self, but rather, "The summons [of Jesus] was away from a life centered in the self . . . to a new life centered in God."[93]

He attempted to equate the different religions on the grounds of overcoming self-centeredness as follows:

The path laid out in the Indian traditions is that of a progressive deconstruction of the ego-boundaries. That developed within the Semitic traditions involves the perfecting of the individual self in relationship to God. But this latter in the end does not mean the separate perfecting of distinct atomic entities. For personality is essentially inter-personal, human perfecting consisting in a total self-giving, or islam, to God and a consequent transcendence of the ego boundaries. Thus the eastern and western paths constitute different forms of self-transcendence in response to the Real.[94]

He could not say that if he acknowledged the pervasive and powerful image throughout Scripture of God's role as father, having a parental relationship with each of his children. Instead, Hick dismissed "the maleness of God as thought and

---

[92] *Id.*, page 41.
[93] *Id.*, page 45.
[94] *Id.*, page 356.

experienced within the Semitic traditions" as merely a characteristic that "reflects and validates the patriarchal human societies whose traditions they are."[95]

He would have to acknowledge the eternal importance of the ego if he recognized that the Bible does not merely characterize God as a father but extensively and richly describes God and believers as a family in which each believer is an individual family member relating to God as a child relates to their father and relating to other believers as brothers and sisters. That is vividly expressed in John 14:2, in which Jesus said His Father's house has many mansions. Ego boundaries are essential to those relationships, as depicted in the image of a mansion for every child.

Christians do seek unity. Jesus directed, "Abide in me, and I in you" (John 15:4). Paul professed to follow that command, saying, "I live; yet not I, but Christ liveth in me" (Galatians 2:20). Smith and Hick cite Paul's statement as evidence of "his own form of God-centredness"[96] and "release from the cramping confines of the ego," in which "the circle of self was broken."[97]

However, that unity is not a negating of ego boundaries. Jesus described that unity in His prayer to His Father:

> Neither pray I for these alone, but for them also which shall believe on me . . . that they all may be one; as thou, Father, art in me, and I in thee, that they also may be one in us: that the world may believe that thou hast sent me. And the glory which thou gave me I have given them; that they may be one, even as we are one: I in them, and thou in me, that they

---

[95] *Id.*, page 202.
[96] *Id.*, page 45.
[97] Smith, *op cit.*, page 317.

may be made perfect in one; and that the world may know that thou hast sent me, and hast loved them as thou hast loved me (John 17:20-23).

The model for that unity is the Trinity, in which three distinct Persons are one. All believers are one, and Jesus is one with each of them, similarly to how God the Father is in Jesus. The unity is the fatherly love of God, which is expressed between and among distinct individuals.

Paul spoke several other times of the unity, in addition to his identifying with Jesus in Galatians 2. Each time, he emphasized that it is a unity of many parts that maintain their distinctiveness.

Speaking of diverse spiritual gifts, Paul said, "For as we have many members in one body, and all members have not the same office: so we, being many, are one body in Christ, and every one members one of another" (Romans 12:4-5).

In 1 Corinthians, he used the same metaphor to address the diversity of gifts: "For by one Spirit are we all baptized into one body, whether we be Jews or Gentiles, whether we be bond or free" (1 Corinthians 12:13).

In Galatians he repeated the theme of equality through identity with Jesus: "There is neither Jew nor Greek, there is neither bond nor free, there is neither male nor female: for ye are all one in Christ Jesus" (Galatians 3:28).

Paul said of the taking into their bodies of Jesus' body through communion: "For we being many are one bread, and one body: for we are all partakers of that one bread" (1 Corinthians 10:17). Again, he emphasized the continuing diversity within the unity, saying, "We being many are one."

Luke described the same phenomenon in Acts, saying, "And the multitude of them that believed were of one heart and of one soul" (Acts 4:32). The multitude were joined by a single purpose and a common faith.

Norman Douty described the unity this way:

> As each person is joined to Christ by the incoming of the Holy Spirit, it necessarily follows that all those who are thus united to Him, are also united to one another. The many members constitute one body, the many stones one temple, and the many descendants one race.[98]

Despite the unity, the individuals continue to exist as members, stones, and descendants. That individuality continues into eternity. Daniel said:

> *And many of them that sleep in the dust of the earth shall awake, some to everlasting life, and some to shame and everlasting contempt. And they that be wise shall shine as the brightness of the firmament; and they that turn many to righteousness as the stars for ever and ever* (Daniel 12:2-3).

Jesus told one of the men crucified with Him, "Verily, I say unto thee, today shalt thou be with me in paradise" (Luke 23:43). Inhabitants of paradise relate to each other and Jesus as individuals. In his vision, John saw individuals in the New Jerusalem: "His servants shall serve him: and they shall see his face; and his name shall be in their foreheads" (Revelation 22:3-4).

Ego boundaries are not destroyed in Christianity. The eastern and western paths do not constitute different forms of self-transcendence. The Christian lives a life centered on God, both in this world and eternity, but it is the life of an individual person, relating to God as an individual Being.

---

[98] Norman Douty, *Union With Christ*, Reiner Publications 1973 edition, page 238.

Therefore, the fatherhood of God demonstrates that the different religions are not merely different paths to the same truth. Buddhism recognizes that, by characterizing belief in a permanent self as one of the "wrong views," they move one to a lower level rather than upward to liberation. Patrul Rinpoche says:

> The term "wrong views" includes, in general, eternalist and nihilist beliefs, which are views contrary to, and outside, the teaching of the Buddha . . . Eternalists believe in a permanent self and an eternally existing creator of the universe . . . From the moment your mind is defiled by false views, even the good you do no longer leads to liberation.[99]

Understanding Christians as children of God in this life and eternally reveals that Christianity and Buddhism do not present "parallel salvific transformations of human life." On the contrary, Christian salvation, which consists of relating to God forever as a child of God, is a Buddhist path to lower realms. The fatherhood of God demonstrates that Christianity is entirely incompatible with Hinduism and Buddhism.

---

[99] Patrul Rinpoche, *The Words of My Perfect Teacher*, Shambhala Publications 1998 edition, pages 21, 110, 112.

23

SALVATION BY WORKS

The characterization throughout the Bible of God as Father and of the House of God paints a vivid picture of God. It reveals Him to those who previously did not know Him and enriches His relationships with those who did know Him but had much to learn. It also enhances the relationships of His children with each other and provides a context for examining various issues of biblical living.

Some people believe that one earns salvation through one's own will and effort in doing the works of God. The Bible tells us otherwise, and those people would see their error if they understood the family of God. The only way to join a family through any effort or will of your own is through marriage. The images of marriage involving God in Scripture do not include individual believers.

John the Baptist described Jesus as a Bridegroom and described himself as a friend of the Bridegroom, saying:

> *He that hath the bride is the bridegroom: but the friend of the bridegroom, which standeth and heareth him, rejoiceth greatly because of the bridegroom's voice: this my joy therefore is fulfilled* (John 3:29).

Jesus compared Himself to a bridegroom and His disciples to friends of the bridegroom (Luke 5:34). Jesus' bride is the church. Paul instructed husbands, "Love your wives, even as

Christ also loved the church, and gave himself for it" (Ephesians 5:25). Paul told the church at Corinth, "I have espoused you to one husband, that I may present you as a chaste virgin to Christ" (2 Corinthians 11:2). Therefore, although marriage is a way into a human family, it is not a way into the family of God. We come into the family of God not as spouses but as children.

Jesus called the process of joining the family of God being "born of the Spirit" (John 3:5-8). John called it being "born, not of blood, nor of the will of the flesh, nor of the will of man, but of God" (John 1:13). Peter called it being "born again, not of corruptible seed, but of incorruptible, by the word of God" (1 Peter 1:23).

Paul also spoke of joining the family of God through the Spirit, but he called it "the Spirit of adoption whereby we cry, Abba, Father" (Romans 8:15). He called the process "the adoption of children by Jesus Christ to himself, according to the good pleasure of his will" (Ephesians 1:5). The hymn writer Hattie Buell elaborated on Paul's imagery in "The Child of a King," praising God for adopting her:

I once was an outcast stranger on earth, a sinner by choice, and an alien by birth! But I've been adopted, my name's written down, an heir to a mansion, a robe and a crown.

Becoming children of God, whether by birth or adoption, is done only through the will of the Father.

The Father-child relationship of God to believers should alone rule out any possibility of people working their way into a relationship with God. However, God expressly made that clear throughout the New Testament.

Paul told the Romans that becoming children of God "is not of him that willeth, nor of him that runneth, but of God that sheweth mercy" (Romans 9:16). The will of God makes it happen. The believer's will plays no part. Elsewhere he told the Romans that "a man is justified by faith without the deeds of the law" (Romans 3:28), and he called works a stumbling stone (Romans 9:32). He said to the Ephesians, "By grace are ye saved through faith: and that not of yourselves: it is the gift of God: not of works, lest anyone should boast" (Ephesians 2:8-9). He told Timothy that God "hath saved us, and called us with an holy calling, not according to our works, but according to his own purpose and grace" (2 Timothy 1:9). He told Titus, "not by works of righteousness which we have done, but according to his mercy he saved us ... that being justified by his grace, we should be made heirs according to the hope of eternal life" (Titus 3:5-7). He told the Philippians, "Work out your own salvation with fear and trembling," explaining, "for it is God which worketh in you" (Philippians 2:12-13).

In "Rock of Ages," Augustus Toplady restated Paul's theme that God has saved us not according to our works:

> Not the labors of my hands can fulfill thy law's demands;
> could my zeal no respite know, could my tears forever flow,
> all for sin could not atone; thou must save, and thou alone.

Jesus said, in the Sermon on the Mount, "Love ye your enemies, and do good ... hoping for nothing again [in return] ... and ye shall be the children of the Highest ... Be ye therefore merciful, as your Father also is merciful" (Luke 6:35-36). He was not saying that doing good would make them sons of God, for He identified God as their Father, regardless of whether they followed His direction to do good. Instead, He was saying that doing good would fulfill their roles as children of God.

Jesus made it clear that salvation is solely the work of God.

His disciples, amazed at His saying a camel could go through the eye of a needle more easily than a rich man could enter the kingdom of God, asked Him, "Who then can be saved?" Jesus answered, "With men this is impossible; but with God all things are possible" (Matthew 19:24-26).

Some of the five thousand whom Jesus had miraculously fed with five barley loaves and two small fishes followed Him and asked Him, "What shall we do, that we might work the works of God?" (John 6:28). Jesus answered that it is not a question of what they do but what God does.

He began by telling them that believing in Him is working the work of God. They asked Him for a sign that they may see and believe. They suggested a sign like God's sending bread from heaven as manna to their ancestors in the desert. When Jesus told them He was the Bread of Life, come down from heaven, they murmured against Him, asking themselves how that man, whose parents they knew, could have come down from heaven. Jesus told them to stop murmuring and explained their disbelief by telling them, "No man can come to me, except the Father which hath sent me draw him," and again, "But there are some of you that believe not . . . Therefore said I unto you, that no man can come unto me, except it were given unto him of my Father" (John 6:44, 64-65).

Jesus also said, "No man knoweth . . . who the Father is, but the Son, and he to whom the Son will reveal him" (Luke 10:22). When Simon Peter said Jesus was "the Christ, the Son of the living God," Jesus said, "Flesh and blood hath not revealed it unto thee, but my Father which is in heaven" (Matthew 16:17).

Acts 2:47 says, "The Lord added to the church daily such as should be saved." When Paul and Barnabas preached in

Antioch, "as many as were ordained to eternal life believed" (Acts 13:48). Acts also describes the believers in Achaia whom Apollos helped as having "believed through grace" (Acts 18:27).

Despite those repeated statements that we are brought into a relationship with God by the grace of God and not by our works, many continue to preach salvation by works. In doing so, they disregard those statements and the nature of a believer's relationship with God as a Father. One cannot work one's way into the family of God any more than one could will oneself to become the child of one's human father.

Kierkegaard said this about works in the context of children relating to a father:

> Good works in the sense of meritoriousness are naturally an abomination to God. Yet works are required of a human being. But they shall be and yet shall not be; they shall be and yet one ought humbly to be ignorant of their being or that they shall have any significance ... it is as when a child gives his parents a present procured, however, with what the child has received from his parents; all the pretentiousness which otherwise resides in giving a gift disappears when the child has received from his parents the gift which he gives to the parents.[100]

---

[100] Soren Kierkegaard, *Works of Love*, Harper & Row, 1962, pages 377 – 378, n. 88.

24

THE NUCLEAR FAMILY

God's choosing to explain Himself to us in the metaphors of Father and the house of God shows that family relationships are important to us and valued by God. The relative importance of the nuclear family, the extended family, the tribe, and the community have changed over time, and some people caution about further change. Some assert that the nuclear family is, and should be maintained as, a Christian institution.

Yuval Noah Harari, in examining happiness, says:

Family and community seem to have more impact on our happiness than money and health. People with strong families who live in tight-knit and supportive communities are significantly happier than people whose families are dysfunctional and who have never found (or never sought) a community to be part of.[101]

Change to family structure appears to be underway. A study of "Marital Alternatives: Extended Groups in Modern Society" by Larry and Joan Constantine says:

In various ways, the family is being extended beyond its traditional boundaries (indeed, the boundaries may be blurring altogether) . . . [I]ncreasing interest in sodalities and extended groups of all kinds, including group marriages,

---

101 Yuval Noah Harari, *Sapiens*, Harper Perennial, 2018, page 382.

family networks, encounter groups, and communes, is a functional adaptation.[102]

Robert Bellah described movement in American social patterns toward collectives (including churches), communes, and extended families, which he called the earth tradition. He contrasted that with the American Protestant tradition as follows:

> Socially the earth tradition expresses itself not through impersonal bureaucracy or the isolated nuclear family but through collectives, communes, tribes and large extended families.[103]

Yuval Noah Harari believes we have moved even beyond that. He proposes that:

> Prior to the Industrial Revolution, the daily life of most humans ran its course within three ancient frames: the nuclear family, the extended family and the local intimate community . . . All this changed over the last two centuries . . . Over time, states and markets used their growing power to weaken the traditional bonds of family and community . . . Markets and states today provide most of the material needs once provided by communities, but they must also supply tribal bonds. Markets and states do so by fostering "imagined communities" . . . which are tailored to national and commercial needs.[104]

Allan Bloom praised the family and warned of the danger of losing that bond:

---

[102] Larry Constantine and Joan Constantine, *Contemporary Marriage: Structure, Dynamics, and Therapy*, Little, Brown and Company, 1976, page 54.

[103] Robert Bellah, *The Broken Covenant*, The Seabury Press, 1975, page 160.

[104] Yuval Noah Harari, *Sapiens*, Harper Perennial, 2018, pages 356-362.

The important lesson that the family taught was the existence of the only unbreakable bond, for better or for worse, between human beings.

The decomposition of this bond is surely America's most urgent social problem.[105]

The Rev. Jerry Falwell focused on the nuclear family, characterizing it as a Christian institution. He called for "preserving our cherished family heritage," defining "family" as follows:

The family is the God-ordained institution of the marriage of one man and one woman together for a lifetime with their biological or adopted children. The family is the fundamental building block and the basic unit of our society.[106]

However, modern Christians who argue for "traditional family values" based on a model of a nuclear family with a father, a mother, and their children must look elsewhere than the Bible to find justification for that model. The family model throughout the Bible is a patriarchal, extended family that is more a family business than the effort of two parents to rear children to maturity.

Old Testament families were often polygamous, and in the New Testament, Paul's marry-if-you-must directive[107] was hardly an inspiration to participate in producing a nuclear family. Also, in the New Testament, we read of Mary, Martha, and Lazarus (two sisters and a brother), the center of a nuclear

---

[105] Allan Bloom, *The Closing of the American Mind*, page 119.

[106] Jerry Falwell, *Listen, America!*, Doubleday & Company, Inc. 1980 edition, page 120.

[107] "I say therefore to the unmarried and to the widows, it is good for them if they abide even as I [single]. But if they cannot contain, let them marry: for it is better to marry than to burn [with passion]" (1 Corinthians 7:8-9).

family. We hear nothing of their parents orbiting that nucleus, and all three appear to be single, doing nothing to create nuclear families of their own.[108]

Anyone wishing to attribute social problems to ignoring biblical family values misunderstands those values if one traces the problems to an increase in single parents. One would come closer to the biblical model if one traced the problems to an increase in the separation of nuclear families from their extended families of grandparents, aunts, uncles, and cousins. A single parent in close contact with and supported by his or her extended family follows the biblical model better than a nuclear family that moves to California and visits the extended family in Ohio once or twice a year.

Changes in family structure may be cause for concern. Still, a call for maintaining the nuclear family as a Christian institution is not supported by the biblical model of the family.

---

[108] See John 11:1-44; 12:1-11.

25

LEGISLATING RELIGIOUS RULES

Some American Christians attempt to enforce Christian mores through the political system. In the United States of America, their influence grew to the point that they became identified as the Christian right. Jerry Falwell called for political action with these words:

> We as American Citizens must recommit ourselves to the faith of our fathers and to the premises and moral foundations upon which this country was established . . . The authority of the Bible must once again be recognized as the legitimate guiding principle of our nation.[109]

Christian nationalists, a subgroup of the Christian right, "focus on . . . passing laws that reflect their view of Christianity and its role in political and social life," according to Wikipedia, which provides the example of blue laws that restrict activities on Sundays.

Christians in other countries have done the same. The *Los Angeles Times* reported on June 7, 2004, that Adelor Vieira, a Brazilian congressperson, "is determined to ensure that Brazil's statute book reflect the principles of the Good Book." It further reported that evangelical Christians in Brazil formed an official

---

[109] Jerry Falwell *Listen, America!*, Doubleday & Company, Inc. 1980 edition, page 265.

lobby in Congress called the Evangelical Parliamentary Front, whose goal is to make public policy fall "in line with God's purposes, and according to His Word." The Evangelical Parliamentary Front was influential in the 2018 presidential election.

The use of political power by God's children to make others behave as though they were members of the house of God is contrary to biblical example and is inconsistent with the concept of the house of God. In the Bible, those with governmental power or the potential for political power have not used it to enforce God's law.

Jesus was suspected of seeking political power and had opportunities to exercise it but rejected it. When He saw that the people were about to make Him king, He fled to a mountain (John 6:15). Later, He told Pilate that His kingdom was not of this world. His servants would have fought for Him if it had been of this world (John 18:36).

Joseph, Daniel, Esther, and Mordecai each had a position of considerable influence in a secular government. None of them used that position to make nonbelievers behave in a godly way. Daniel influenced King Darius to make a decree honoring Jehovah as the living God (Daniel 6:26), but he did not do it through his political office. Instead, he did it by setting an example through his behavior. Esther and Mordecai used their positions only to protect the interests of the Jew (see Esther 8:16; 10:3). In response to Esther and Mordecai's actions, many people converted to Judaism (Esther 8:17). Although godliness increased because of their efforts, it was because they first turned the people around spiritually.

The Lord said, through Jeremiah, that He would refrain from punishing a nation if it changed its behavior. He said, "If that nation, against whom I have pronounced, turn from their evil, I will repent of the evil that I thought to do unto them" (Jeremiah 18:8). He was not speaking of changing their behavior by changing laws. Turning from evil requires more than better behavior through better rules. It requires a national change of heart.

The Lord determined to scatter Judah "because my people hath forgotten me" (Jeremiah 18:15-17). On the other hand, He spared the people of Nineveh from judgment because "they turned from their evil way" in city-wide repentance (Jonah 3:10). Each group had a spiritual problem. Each required a spiritual solution.

Government was created by Jesus, for Jesus. Paul wrote in Colossians:

For by him were all things created, that are in heaven, and that are in earth, visible and invisible, whether they be thrones, or dominions, or principalities, or powers: all things were created by him, and for him (Colossians 1:16).

God uses government for our good. We presume too much, however, when we take that to mean we should use governments to try to reach religious goals. God directs us to comply with secular laws to further God's purpose. Peter addressed his first epistle to "the strangers scattered throughout Pontus, Galatia, Cappadocia, Asia, and Bithynia" (1 Peter 1:1). They were outsiders in their states of residence as both Jews and Christians. Despite the secularity of those governments, he directed them:

Submit yourselves to every ordinance of man for the Lord's sake: whether it be to the king, as supreme; or unto governors, as unto them that are sent by him for the punishment of evildoers, and for the praise of them that do well . . . Honour all men. Love the brotherhood. Fear God. Honour the king (1 Peter 2:13-17).

Paul told the citizens of Rome, "Rulers are not a terror to good works, but to the evil." He said that the ruler "is the minister of God to thee for good" (Romans 13:3-4). Paul was not telling them that God used Rome's government to enforce obedience of God's standards of behavior. The good that he spoke of is the good of orderliness.

Dietrich Bonhoeffer described government's duty to Jesus, as its creator, as follows:

> Government is instituted for the sake of Christ; it serves Christ, and consequently it also serves the Church. Yet the dominion of Christ over all government does not by any means imply the dominion of the Church over government ... The service of government to Christ consists in the exercise of its commission to secure an outward justice by the power of the sword. This service is thus an indirect service to the congregation, which only by this is enabled to "lead a quiet and peaceable life" (1 Timothy 2:2).[110]

The Church's claim on government "is not that government should pursue a Christian policy, enact Christian laws, etc., but that it should be true government in accordance with its own special task."[111]

The Church's responsibility is not to improve community behavior through political influence but to address individuals' salvation:

> It is part of the Church's office of guardianship that she shall call sin by its name and that she shall warn men against sin ... This warning against sin is delivered to the congregation openly and publicly, and whoever will not hear it passes

---

[110] Dietrich Bonhoeffer, *Ethics*, Macmillan Paperback 1965 edition, page 346.
[111] *Id.*, page 347.

judgment upon himself. The intention of the preacher here is not to improve the world, but to summon it to belief in Jesus Christ and to bear witness to the reconciliation which has been accomplished through Him and to His dominion.[112]

That is not to say that a person acting politically, whether as a voter or government member, should not act following one's faith. Constitutional Law scholar Professor Stephen Carter, writing on the Establishment Clause of the First Amendment of the U. S. Constitution ("Congress shall make no law respecting an establishment of religion"), has argued, "The Establishment Clause . . . must not be allowed to . . . force the religiously devout to bracket their religious selves before they enter into politics."[113] He explained, "The metaphorical separation of church and state originated in an effort to protect religion from the state, not the state from religion."[114]

Similarly, the biblical approach to government, and in particular the approach suggested by the concept of the house of God, does not force such bracketing. God's children should act to please the Father in all they do and should employ the rules and subjective values of the Father both in their deportment and in their governing. As Timothy Keller said, "When you come into the public square it is impossible to leave your convictions about ultimate values behind."[115]

Nonetheless, in participating in the public square, God's children should make a practice of limiting their legislating to

---

[112] *Id.*, page 350.
[113] Stephen Carter, *The Culture of Disbelief*, Basic Books, 1993, pages 254 – 255.
[114] *Id.*, page 105.
[115] Timothy Keller, *The Reason For God,* Dutton, 2008, page 17.

preserving the rights of their brothers and sisters and themselves to live in a way pleasing to the Father. At the same time, they should attempt to preserve the rights of those outside the house of God to stay outside the family and to live free of religious constraints. According to Professor Carter, "[T]here are good reasons, both theological and practical, for all religions to honor the freedom of nonmembers to follow other religions—or to follow no religion at all."[116]

Occasions will occur when spiritual principles can enhance the common good and when spiritual principles will conflict with secular desires at a level of gravity and scope that requires imposing spiritually inspired rules on all, including those outside the house of God. Richard John Neuhaus said, "Christian truth . . . is accessible to public reason . . . At some critical points of morality and ethics it speaks to public policy."[117] Professor Carter gave examples:

> [O]ne reason it should not be surprising that both the nineteenth-century abolitionist movement and the twentieth-century civil rights movement had their origins in the religions is that it is precisely there, in the realm of the religions, where humans search for ultimate meaning, that one is most likely to find the powerful challenge to the meanings that the state seeks to impose."[118]

When that happens, the children of God will be the most faithful to their family relationship and will be most effective if they act outside the halls of power rather than inside.

---

[116] Stephen Carter, *God's Name in Vain*, Basic Books, 2000, page 158.
[117] Richard John Neuhaus, The Naked Public Square, William B. Eerdmans Publishing Company, 1984, page 260.
[118] Stephen Carter, *The Culture of Disbelief*, Basic Books, 1993, page 272.

Professor Carter warned, "The closer the religions move to the center of secular power (as against influence), the less likely they are to discover meanings that are in competition with those imposed by the state."[119]

Not only is there a danger of losing perspective by establishing power, but there is also a danger of a backlash from nonbelievers. Richard John Neuhaus illustrated that with a story:

> At his inauguration in 1978, Pope John Paul I refused to be crowned with the papal tiara, the vestigial symbol of the claim to temporal power. John Paul II followed his example, and so must all the churches set aside their tiaras, not even keeping them in the closet but destroying them altogether. It may seem unwarranted to us, but there are many secularists in this society (and many believers) who do most genuinely fear the church's ambitions to rule. Those fears must be put to rest if we are ever to achieve a more natural and fruitful relationship between church and state, between religion and the public square.[120]

After His resurrection, before giving His Great Commission, Jesus told His disciples, "All power is given unto me in heaven and in earth" (Matthew 28:18). Yet, even with that introduction, He did not commission them to change the nation's governments. Instead, He commissioned them to "teach all nations, baptizing them in the name of the Father, and of the Son, and of the Holy Ghost" (Matthew 28:19).

Baptizing people in the name of the Father, the Son, and the Holy Spirit recognizes that they have been "born of the

---

[119] Id., page 273.
[120] Richard John Neuhaus, The Naked Public Square, William B. Eerdmans Publishing Company, 1984, page 260.

Spirit," (John 3:5-8), which brought them into the family of God. Within the family of God, they will encounter God's standards of behavior in a spiritual setting. Refraining from exercising political power to enforce those practices evident throughout the Bible is understood best in the context of the house of God. Only His children can fully understand God's standards, and only through understanding them can anyone follow them to the satisfaction of the Father. Following the rules is obedience to the Father. It is a family matter.

26

ASCETICISM

Grace notwithstanding, Christians rightly emphasize the importance of godly behavior. We all should sing with conviction the words of Robert Robinson in "Come, Thou Fount of Every Blessing:"

> O to grace how great a debtor daily I'm constrained to be; let that grace now, like a fetter, bind my wand'ring heart to thee. Prone to wander, Lord, I feel it, prone to leave the God I love; here's my heart, O take and seal it, seal it for Thy courts above.

However, some Christians slip from a desire for godly behavior into an attitude that we are unworthy of pleasure. They follow a legalism in which our worthiness is based on our compliance with rules. Because of the accurate conviction that we are all sinners, falling short of God's commandments, that legalism leads naturally to the inaccurate conclusion that we are not worthy of pleasure.

Prominent believers throughout the Old and New Testaments provide impressive examples of enduring hardship. During the drought, Elijah lived off bread brought by ravens and water from a brook (1 Kings 17:1-7). John the Baptist clothed himself with camel's hair and ate locusts and wild honey (Matthew 3:4; Mark 1:6). He neither ate bread nor drank wine, making Jesus look like a "gluttonous man and a winebibber" in contrast (Luke 7:33-34). Paul wrote inspirationally while in prison.

Some Christians look to those saints as models in pursuing asceticism. Few people live in the wild and eat locusts in pursuit of a godly life, but many find other ways of limiting their pleasure and spurning support in times of hardship.

Throughout his letter to the Philippians, Paul described his hardships while talking about joy. Paul told the Philippians that he prayed for them with joy (Philippians 1:4). He said he rejoiced in the preaching of Christ (Philippians 1:18). He urged them to fulfill his joy by being of one accord (Philippians 2:2). He called them his "joy and crown" (Philippians 4:1). He told them he "rejoiced in the Lord greatly" that their care for him had flourished again (Philippians 4:10).

Some commentators cite Philippians, with its many uses of the words *joy* and *rejoice*, to propose that believers should be joyful when facing hardships. James Montgomery Boice called it "The Joyful Letter." He wrote:

> The letter to the Philippians is one of the most joyous books in the Bible. All the way through the letter Paul speaks of joy, of inner happiness ... He had learned to rejoice in whatever state he was. He overflowed with rejoicing ... Think of it—the great apostle in a dirty Roman prison, deserted by most of his friends, and almost forgotten. And yet he writes with joy, rejoicing in the riches that belong to all believers in Christ.[121]

That is not to say we should rejoice in the hardships. The words "and yet" indicate Paul rejoiced despite the hardships. Specifically

---

[121] James Montgomery Boice, *Philippians: An Expositional Commentary*, Zondervan, Grand Rapids, MI, 1976, pages 13-15.

he rejoiced in "the riches that belong to all believers in Christ." Stuart Briscoe went beyond that in his book on Philippians called *Bound For Joy: Philippians—Paul's Letter From Prison.* He titled the first chapter "I'm So Happy Here in Prison." Based on what he saw as Paul's happiness in prison, he challenged the reader as follows:

> When you find yourself in prison, or in a hospital bed, or tied to a kitchen sink, or anchored to an office desk, it's a good thing to remember what God has been doing in your life instead of moaning about your present status.[122]

To say that we should stop moaning and be happy about hardships suggests that it is wrong to grieve or otherwise acknowledge suffering. The Bible tells us otherwise, however, through the examples of David, Jesus, and Paul, and the writings of Peter and James.

David's Psalms show us how to acknowledge our suffering and seek help from our Father. David said, "I cried unto the Lord with my voice . . . I poured out my complaint before Him" (Psalm 142:1-2). When he did not cry out to the Lord in his hardship, he groaned in suffering. He said, "When I kept silence, my bones waxed old through my roaring all the day long" (Psalm 32:3). So cry out he did, many times, in the Psalms. He complained to the Lord about his enemies, and he spoke explicitly and poignantly of his pain:

Lord, how are they increased that trouble me! (Psalm 3:1)

Thou hast enlarged me when I was in distress (Psalm 4:1).

My soul is also sore vexed (Psalm 6:3).

---

122 Stuart Briscoe, *Bound For Joy: Philippians—Paul's Letter From Prison,* G/L Publications, Glendale, CA, 1975, page 4.

I am weary with my groaning; all the night make I my bed to swim; I water my couch with my tears. Mine eye is consumed because of grief (Psalm 6:6-7).

Save me from all them that persecute me (Psalm 7:1).

Consider my trouble which I suffer of them that hate me (Psalm 9:13).

How long shall I take counsel in my soul, having sorrow in my heart daily? (Psalm 13:2)

The sorrows of hell compassed me . . . In my distress I called upon the Lord (Psalm 18:5-6).

I am poured out like water, and all my bones are out of joint: my heart is like wax (Psalm 22:14).

I am desolate and afflicted (Psalm 25:16).

My life is spent with grief, and my years with sighing (Psalm 31:10).

I am troubled; I am bowed down greatly; I go mourning all the day long (Psalm 38:6).

[M]y sorrow is continually before me (Psalm 38:17).

I am poor and needy (Psalms 40:17, 70:5, 86:1; 109:22).

My heart is sore pained within me: and the terrors of death are fallen upon me. Fearfulness and trembling are come upon me, and horror hath overwhelmed me (Psalm 55:4-5).

I am weary of my crying: my throat is dried: Mine eyes fail while I wait for my God (Psalm 69:3).

Reproach hath broken my heart; and I am full of heaviness (Psalm 69:20).

I am poor and sorrowful (Psalm 69:29).

I poured out my complaint before him; I shewed before him my trouble (Psalm 142:2).

Therefore is my spirit overwhelmed within me; my heart within me is desolate (Psalm 143:4).

Jesus suffered horribly on the cross and at the hands of the Roman soldiers. That was a unique event in which Jesus paid the price for our sins as the ultimate sacrificial Lamb, but Jesus is nonetheless an example to us in expressing His suffering.

As His arrest and crucifixion approached, He was deeply distressed and in agony (Matthew 26:37; Mark 14:33; Luke 22:44). He described Himself as "exceeding sorrowful" (Matthew 26:38; Mark 14:34). He asked His Father to take the cup away from Him if it was His will (Matthew 26:29, 42, 44; Mark 14:35-36, 39; Luke 22:42). As He prayed, "His sweat was as it were great drops of blood falling down to the ground" (Luke 22:44).

Isaiah described the Messiah as "a man of sorrows, and acquainted with grief" (Isaiah 53:3). When Jesus' close friend Lazarus died, Jesus "groaned in the spirit, and was troubled" (John 11:33). Jesus openly acknowledged His suffering, weeping over Lazarus' death, causing some witnesses to comment on His love for Lazarus and others to question why He had not prevented the death with His healing powers.

Peter said Jesus was a model to us in His suffering (1 Peter 2:21) but not by denying His anguish. Instead, the example of Jesus was that "when he suffered, He threatened not" (1 Peter 2:23).

Paul was not as happy to be in prison as some commentators make him out to have been. Many of Paul's uses of the words *joy* and *rejoice* refer not to his joy but the joy of the Philippians (Philippians 1:25-26, 2:28, 3:1; 4:4). Even the references to his joy do not refer to his hardships, with two exceptions, but to his joy in the unity of the Philippians, their care for him, and his joy in praying for them.

Paul's first reference to the joy that pertained to his hardships was his reaction to his imprisonment's resulting in more preaching. He observed that, "Many of the brethren in the Lord, waxing confident by my bonds, are much more bold to speak the word without fear," and that "some indeed preach Christ even ... supposing to add affliction to my bonds." Paul's reaction was "whether in pretense, or in truth, Christ is preached; and I therein do rejoice, yea, and will rejoice" (Philippians 1:14-18). Although that joy related to Paul's hardships, it was not joy in the pain of the difficulties. It was in the preaching that he rejoiced, not the chains. Paul emphasized that he rejoiced in the preaching despite the painful cause.

Paul's second reference to joy that pertained to hardships was his statement, "If I be offered upon the sacrifice and service of your faith, I joy, and rejoice with you all" (Philippians 2:17). Again, he rejoiced in the result, not the painful cause, and contrasted the good of the result with the bad of the cause. He encouraged them to rejoice with him because of the excellent result, despite the suffering.

His comments on his hardships indicate his sorrow, not joy, about those hardships. Paul's letter to the Philippians is full of frank descriptions of bad experiences and the pain they caused.

In chapter one, he spoke in verse 7 of his chains and in verse 8 of his great longing for the Philippians. In verses 12 through 18, he described justification for "the things which happened unto me." In verses 19 through 26, he said he wished he could die, "to depart, and to be with Christ." In verses 27 through 30 he called on the Philippians to exercise courage in the face of adversaries and suffering.

In chapter two, in verse 1, he spoke of consolation and comfort, which are relief from sorrow. In verse 16, he expressed concern about laboring in vain. In verse 27, he said God had mercy on him "lest I should have sorrow upon sorrow." In verse 28 he said he sent Epaphroditus to them so that he "may be less sorrowful."

In chapter three, in verse 13, he said he was "forgetting those things which are behind, and reaching forth unto those things which are before." His desire was to put the bad experiences behind him.

Finally, in chapter four, in verses 11 and 12, he said, "I have learned, in whatsoever state I am, therewith to be content. I know ... how to be abased ....I am instructed both to be full and to be hungry, both to abound and to suffer need." The word translated "content" is better translated "self-sufficient" or "resourceful." Paul describes his self-sufficiency in verses 12 and 13 as "knowing how" to be abased and to abound, and being able to do all things, although he acknowledges that his resources come from above. Paul describes tolerating hardship by virtue of his ability to adapt, with God's help.

Those who preach that Paul tells us in Philippians to rejoice in our hardships take Paul's use of the words *joy* and *rejoice* out of context and ignore the tone of suffering and longing in the epistle.

Paul told the Corinthians, "I take pleasure in infirmities, in reproaches, in necessities, in persecutions, in distresses for Christ's sake: for when I am weak, then am I strong" (2 Corinthians 12:10). Paul's speaking of pleasure in hardships at first hearing sounds as though Paul rejoiced in hardship, but he was actually seeking consolation for a disagreeable circumstance.

Although Paul said in verse 10 that he took pleasure in infirmities, reproaches, necessities, and persecutions, the context shows that he suffered when he experienced those difficulties. Furthermore, it shows that he would have greatly preferred to attain his goals without those difficulties.

In verse 8, Paul said that he "besought the Lord thrice" that the Lord would cure his physical problem. That makes clear that Paul strongly wished to be relieved of the problem and took pleasure only in the extent to which his suffering worked for Christ's sake and served to make him stronger. In verse 10, in saying, "I take pleasure . . . in distresses," he acknowledged that he felt distress. When Paul was ill, attacked, and lacked what he needed, he was not oblivious to the pain and incapacity. It hurt him, and he suffered from it, and he prayed for relief.

Likewise, Peter spoke of taking pleasure in the result while granting the grief of enduring the hardship in his first epistle:

Wherein ye greatly rejoice, though now for a season, if need be, ye are in heaviness through manifold temptations: that the trial of your faith, being much more precious than of gold that perisheth, though it be tried with fire, might be found unto praise and honour and glory at the appearing of Jesus Christ (1 Peter 1:6-7).

James said nearly the same thing:

My brethren, count it all joy when ye fall into divers temptations; knowing this, that the trying of your faith worketh patience (James 1:2).

The rejoicing looks ahead to the growth that will be gained. The natural and appropriate emotional response to the experience of the trials is grief, not joy. James tells us to "count it" joy because we do not automatically feel joy.

Peter also spoke of rejoicing in the suffering we experience because we are Christians. He told us to "rejoice, inasmuch as ye are partakers of Christ's sufferings; that when his glory shall be revealed, ye may be glad also with exceeding joy" (1 Peter 4:13). He said that a person suffering as a Christian should "not be ashamed, but . . . glorify God" (1 Peter 4:16). Peter recognized the pain of the suffering and did not counsel us to ignore the pain or to pretend that it was not there. Instead, he encouraged us to look ahead and rejoice in the outcome.

Rejoicing in the result does not eliminate the real grief in the trials. The trials should not be sought out but endured "if need be." In telling people they should rejoice in suffering, we must be careful not to suggest that they should welcome suffering, which would ignore that it is to be endured "if need be" and that we are justified in asking the Lord to remove the adversity.

Remember Jesus' comment about John the Baptist's neither eating bread nor drinking wine. He said people compared Him to John the Baptist and called Him a "gluttonous man and a winebibber" (Luke 7:33-34). The scribes and the Pharisees also asked Him why John the Baptist's followers often fasted while Jesus' followers "eat and drink" (Luke 5:33). Jesus excused His disciples for celebrating His presence among them and did not apologize for His eating and drinking. Instead, He said, "Wisdom is justified of all her children," and then accepted a Pharisee's invitation to eat with him (Luke 7:35-36).

To believe that we are unworthy of pleasure or freedom from suffering is to see only the Father who requires the performance of difficult tasks by His children and who disciplines them when they fail or when they need discipline to grow. Philippians and 2 Corinthians 12:10 help us accept those demands and that discipline. But we should not read them as some do, ignoring the loving nature of that Father, who takes pleasure in the happiness of His children.

In the Sermon on the Mount, Jesus described our heavenly Father as generous to His children, as follows:

> *Ask, and it shall be given you; seek, and ye shall find; knock, and it shall be opened unto you: For every one that asketh receiveth; and he that seeketh findeth; and to him that knocketh it shall be opened. Or what man is there of you, whom if his son ask bread, will he give him a stone? Of if he ask a fish, will he give him a serpent? If ye, then, being evil, know how to give good gifts unto your children, how much more shall your Father which is in heaven give good things to them that ask Him?* (Matthew 7:7-11)

Paul too told us to ask. Rather than advising us to welcome hardship and to reject pleasurable things, he said, "in every thing by prayer and supplication with thanksgiving let your requests be made known unto God" (Philippians 4:6).

James described God as a generous Father who consistently gives good gifts:

> *Every good gift and every perfect gift is from above, and cometh down from the Father of lights, with whom is no variableness, neither shadow of turning* (James 1:17).

In the Sermon on the Mount, while telling us to ask, Jesus described us as evil. Despite that, because of Jesus' death on the cross to atone for our sins, God relates to believers as a loving Father to His children. The legalism of unworthiness sees only the evil and not the forgiveness and concludes that we are not worthy of good things and freedom from pain. That robs God of part of His glory and robs us of the pleasure we should have from fully enjoying the love of our Father.

Understanding God as our Father shows us that it pleases

God, as it pleases any father, to provide for His children. We should not presume to detract from that.

27

How Many Mansions?

How large, then, is the house of God? How many mansions does it hold? Who exactly are the children of God? If Allah is not God, and Hinduism and Buddhism are inconsistent with Christianity, are followers of those religions outside the family of God? Only about 30 percent of people profess to be Christian, and many may make a profession of faith that others believe is not genuine. Even if making a profession of faith were the standard, while that would be a large family, currently, twice as many would be excluded as would be included.

Jesus told even a group of Jews, who believed they were in God's family as descendants of Abraham, that those who rejected Him were not in God's family:

Jesus saith unto them, If ye were Abraham's children, ye would do the works of Abraham. But now ye seek to kill me, a man that hath told you the truth, which I have heard of God: This did not Abraham. Ye do the deeds of your father. Then said they to him, We be not born of fornication; we have one Father, even God. Jesus said unto them, If God were your Father, ye would love me: for I proceeded forth and came from God . . . Ye are of your father the devil, and the lusts of your father ye will do (John 8:39-44).

In the Old Testament, God declared His nature and His relationship to humankind when, on Mount Sinai with Moses, God proclaimed His name:

The LORD, The LORD God [Jehovah, Jehovah Elohim], merciful and gracious, long-suffering, and abundant in goodness and truth, keeping mercy for thousands, forgiving iniquity and transgression and sin, and that will by no means clear the guilty; visiting the iniquity of the fathers upon the children, and upon the children's children, unto the third and to the fourth generation (Exodus 34:6-7).

In that proclamation of His name, the Lord went straight to the essential tension of His relationship with human beings when He said He is "forgiving iniquity and transgressions and sin, and . . . will by no means clear the guilty." He emphasized forgiveness by stating it in three ways, and He emphasized judgment by qualifying "clear the guilty" with "by no means."

That tension between judgment and mercy appears throughout the New Testament. The many expressions of that tension further show its central role in our relationship with God. For example, Jesus said that "not everyone that saith unto me, Lord, Lord, shall enter into the kingdom of Heaven" (Matthew 7:21) and warned of damnation elsewhere in Matthew and throughout the Gospels. However, He also said, "It is not the will of your Father which is in heaven, that one of these little ones should perish," (Matthew 18:14), and "I . . . will draw all men unto me" (John 12:32).

The tension appears in a single statement by Jesus to Nicodemus. Jesus said, "He that believeth not is condemned," in John 3:18, but he also said in the previous verse God sent Him "that the world through him might be saved." It similarly appeared in a single statement to Sadducees who challenged Him on the resurrection. In Luke 20:35-38, Jesus referred to "they which shall be accounted worthy," implying some will be accounted worthy and some will not, and three verses later, He said God is "a God . . . of the living, for all live unto Him."

Paul told the Romans that God "will render . . . tribulation and anguish, upon every soul of man that doeth evil," in Romans 2:6-9, a grim forecast of punishment. However, he also told them, "As by the offense of one judgment came upon all men to condemnation; even so by the righteousness of one the free gift came upon all men unto justification of life" (Romans 5:18). That eliminates punishment for everyone because Jesus endured it for them.

Similarly, Paul told the Corinthians, "We must all appear before the judgment seat of Christ" (2 Corinthians 5:10), but also said, "He died for all" (2 Corinthians 5:15). He emphasized salvation for all when he added, "God was in Christ reconciling the world unto himself, not imputing their trespasses unto them" (2 Corinthians 5:19).

Peter too warned of "the day of judgment and perdition of ungodly men" (2 Peter 3:7) but said two verses later that God "is longsuffering to usward, not willing that any should perish, but that all should come to repentance" (2 Peter 3:9).

That tension gets little discussion in the Christian church today, but God expressed it repeatedly through Jesus, Paul, and Peter and used it to characterize Himself when He declared His name.

The complexity of that tension in Scripture increases when Jesus speaks of salvation in the fifth Chapter of John. There, Jesus gives at least two, and possibly three, different pictures of salvation within the space of six verses: that is, those who are spiritually dead but come to believe will be saved (verse 24), and the physically dead will be saved or condemned according to their works (verses 28 and 29). Further, consider verse 25, "the dead shall hear the voice of the Son of God: and they that hear shall live." Adding no inference to those words, that verse means all who are spiritually dead will be saved. However, it could be taken to be a shortened restatement of verse 24, leaving out some key words that are meant to be inferred. Here is what He said:

Verily, verily, I say unto you, he that heareth my word, and believeth on him that sent me, hath everlasting life, and shall not come into condemnation; but is passed from death unto life. Verily, verily, I say unto you, the hour is coming, and now is, when the dead shall hear the voice of the Son of God: and they that hear shall live . . . Marvel not at this: for the hour is coming, in which all that are in the graves shall hear his voice, and shall come forth; they that have done good, unto the resurrection of life; and they that have done evil, unto the resurrection of damnation (John 5:24-29).

Perhaps the apparent contradiction can be understood by examining the timing of Jesus' statements, as may be hinted by Jesus' references to "the hour is coming." At that time in history, Jesus (and humankind with Him) was approaching the juncture of human attempts to fulfill the Law and God's providing the perfect atonement through the perfect sacrifice. Jesus could, at that point in time, choose to judge (as He said in verse 30, "My judgment is just"). If He judged, His judgment being just, He would condemn under the rule of the Law. Or, instead, He could choose to die as the perfect Lamb of God and save humankind by being the perfect atonement.

At that point in history, when Jesus had that conversation in Jerusalem, Jesus had not yet prayed in the Garden of Gethsemane that the cup be taken from Him. Whether Jesus would go to the cross still hung in the balance. If He had chosen not to go to the cross, or if God had taken that cup from Him and released Him from that mission, a different alternative would have played out.

Following Jesus' entry into Jerusalem on Palm Sunday, Jesus spoke of the critical point in history, "this hour," and the wrenching difficulty of His decision:

> *The hour is come, that the Son of Man should be glorified . . .*
> *Now my soul is troubled; and what shall I say? Father save me*
> *from this hour: but for this cause came I unto this hour* (John 12:23, 27).

After a voice spoke from heaven, Jesus said,

> *Now is the judgment of this world: now the prince of this world*
> *will be cast out. And I, if I be lifted up from the earth, will draw*
> *all men unto me* (John 12:31-32).

The Greek word translated *if*, which is εἰ, can have the conditional connotation usually associated with *if*, but it can also have the meaning of "since," so one should not conclude that the conditional element of *if* necessarily applies. Nonetheless, *if* seems to be a better choice than *since* in the context of Jesus's questioning, in verse 27, of His future decision. If *if* is the better translation, it is another demonstration that the salvation of all men at that point in time hung in the balance.

Given that God inspired the Bible, it is to be expected that we would read it as a God's-eye view, always considering the future as well as the past. It is easy to forget that God made His revelation in time through the voice of men and women who spoke and wrote in actual moments in history. Reminding ourselves of that can provide a different perspective.

Understanding the alternative paths that existed when Jesus had not yet died on the cross may explain contradictory statements of judgment and grace, all the way back to when God told Moses His name on Mount Sinai.

It does not explain, however, John's report that, even after His death and resurrection, Jesus continued to speak of judgment of sin. He met with the disciples, breathed the Holy Spirit on them, and said, "Whose soever sins ye remit, they are remitted unto them; and whose soever sins ye retain, they are retained" (John 20:23).

Similarly, Paul reported a statement by Jesus after His resurrection framed in terms of the house of God and referred to forgiveness of sins and sanctification by faith in Jesus. Paul reported that, in his conversion on the road to Damascus, Jesus said to him:

> *I have appeared unto thee for this purpose . . . delivering thee from the [Jewish] people, and from the Gentiles, unto whom now I send thee, to open their eyes, and to turn them from darkness to light, and from the power of Satan unto God, that they may receive forgiveness of sins, and inheritance among them which are sanctified by faith that is in me* (Acts 26:16-18).

Understanding the timing also does not explain Revelation, with its references to judgment of works. Examples include:

> *And the dead were judged out of those things which were written in the books, according to their works . . . And they were judged every man according to their works . . .* (Revelation 20:12-13).

> *Blessed are they that do his commandments, that they may have right to the tree of life, and may enter in through the gates into the city* (Revelation 22:14).

Considering the New Testament statements that salvation is not by works, those references to works in Revelation may not concern salvation. They may mean that all people, regardless of salvation, are judged and rewarded accordingly.[123]

Still, we must heed the statements indicating that not all are saved. For example:

And whosoever was not found written in the book of life was cast into the lake of fire (Revelation 20:15).

My reward is with me, to give every man according as his work shall be (Revelation 22:12).

Those references extend to the image of the house of God and the role of God as Father:

He that overcometh shall inherit all things; and I will be his God, and he shall be my son (Revelation 21:7).

References in Acts also should be considered, regarding salvation by belief, which suggest not everyone will be saved. For example, Paul preached in Antioch:

And by him all that believe are justified from all things, from which ye could not be justified by the law of Moses (Acts 13:39).

After reporting that sermon, the narrator, understood to be Luke, added:

And as many as were ordained to eternal life believed (Acts 13:48).

In prison in Philippi, when the prison keeper asked Paul and Silas, "Sirs, what must I do to be saved?" they told him:

Believe on the Lord Jesus Christ, and thou shalt be saved, and thy house (Acts 16: 30-31).

So the apparent contradictions are not fully explained by the timing of the statements. Also, apart from timing, the verses warning of exclusion from salvation and exclusion from

---

[123] Brett Preston, *One Taken*, River Birch Press, p.85

the house of God far outnumber those suggesting that Jesus' atonement applies to all. An excellent compilation and exposition is Brett Preston's *One Taken*.[124] All that leaves strong bases for limited atonement, which has been accepted and preached by great theologians through the ages.

But bases for the hope of unlimited atonement also exist. That would mean that all men and women are adopted into the house of God as God's children. What a wonderful hope that is! It sounds deeply wrong from the point of view of the vindictive, but Jesus addressed that in the Sermon on the Mount when He scolded those who judge others:

> *Thou hypocrite, first cast out the beam out of thine own eye; and then shalt thou see clearly to cast out the mote out of thy brother's eye* (Matthew 7:5).

Even if there are bases for the hope of unlimited atonement, we should not let that prospect make us complacent.

God's forgiving sin does not make Him hate sin any less. Our family obligation is to please our Father and model ourselves on his Son, Jesus. "For we are unto God a sweet savour of Christ" (2 Corinthians 2:15). As Paul said to the Galatians, "If, while we seek to be justified by Christ, we ourselves also are found sinners, is therefore Christ the minister of sin? God forbid" (Galatians 2:17). We should "walk worthy of God, who hath called [us] unto his kingdom and glory" (1 Thessalonians 2:12). Even though God has forgiven us, we must battle against sin. Because God has forgiven us, we must battle against sin. We should "put on the whole armour of God, that [we] may be able to stand against the wiles of the devil" (Ephesians 6:11).

God's continuing emphasis on sin and judgment after

---

[124] Brett Preston, *One Taken*, River Birch Press, 2021.

Jesus' atonement also tells us that we need to understand, ponder, and act upon what would be our due if it were not for Jesus' atonement. Those in the family of God need to understand the responsibility that the act of atonement places on the children of God. As Paul exhorted the Philippians, we should "press toward the mark for the prize of the high calling of God in Christ Jesus" (Philippians 3:14).

That responsibility, which arises out of Jesus' atonement for our sins, as well as Jesus' example as God's Son, includes working diligently to bring others into the family of God so that they can enjoy a family relationship with God and other believers as soon as possible. People should know their Father, love their Father and enjoy His love, and benefit from a relationship with their Father.

After Jesus' death and resurrection, He gave the Great Commission:

> *Go ye therefore, and teach all nations, baptizing them in the name of the Father, and of the Son, and of the Holy Ghost: teaching them to observe all things whatsoever I have commanded you* (Matthew 28:19-20).

To understand that instruction, one needs to understand the meaning of "the name of the Father, and of the Son, and of the Holy Ghost."

In the beginning, God demonstrated the power of language, specifically the significance of names. When God created in Genesis 1, He spoke, "and it was so." The next thing He did was to name what He had created. God said, "Let there be light," and there was light. God separated the light from the darkness, and named them, calling the light "day" and the darkness "night." He continued in that fashion, speaking into being and naming sky, land, and seas. He then spoke into being, without naming, vegetation, the sun and moon, and living creatures.[125]

In the case of creating man, instead of saying, "Let there be," He said, "Let us make man in our image, after our likeness" (Genesis 1:26). The first impression of "our image" and "our likeness" suggests we somehow look like God but remembering that God is both invisible and infinite makes us look elsewhere for the meaning. More likely, it refers, at least in part,[126] to our having the facility of language, along with the consciousness that operates it and that it expresses.[127] Of course, when-ever we say we are like God in some way, we must acknowledge the vast otherness of God; we talk, but we cannot speak anything into being, and we have consciousness but not omniscience. Nonetheless, expressing our consciousness

---

[125] For the significance of language to God, see John 1:1-3: "In the beginning was the Word, and the Word was with God, and the Word was God. The same was in the beginning with God. All things were made by him; and without him was not anything made that was made."

[126] See the discussion of gender in chapter 1.

[127] Scientists recognize man's facility of language, and the requisite cognitive ability, as what sets man apart from other animals but are stumped to find a natural, non-theistic explanation for it. Yuval Noah Harari describes it this way: "About 3.8 billion years ago, on a planet called Earth, certain molecules combined to form particularly large and intricate structures called organisms . . . About 70,000 years ago, organisms belonging to the species *Homo Sapiens* started to form even more elaborate structures called cultures . . . The appearance of new ways of thinking and communicating, between 70,000 and 30,000 years ago, constitutes the Cognitive Revolution. What caused it? We're not sure. The most commonly believed theory argues that accidental genetic mutations changed the inner wiring of the brains of Sapiens . . . We might call it the Tree of Knowledge mutation. Why did it occur in Sapiens' DNA rather than in that of Neanderthals? It was a matter of pure chance, as far as we can tell" (*Sapiens*, HarperCollins Publishers, pp. 3, 21).

through language, as well as other means such as music, positions us "a little lower than the angels, ... crowned ... with glory and honour, . . . [with] dominion over the works of [God's] hands."¹²⁸

After the flood, the people said, "Let us build us a city and a tower, whose top may reach unto heaven; and let us make us a name, lest we be scattered abroad upon the face of the whole earth" (Genesis 11:4). In confounding their language, God both responded to their invoking the power of language and the power of a name in particular and solved the problem of their having violated His commandment at Genesis 9:1 to fill the earth. The people of Babel are famous for their tower, but the point of the tower was to make a name. The people did not get the name they sought because God scattered them.

In contrast, the descendants of Abraham had a great name because God granted it to them. In His covenant with Abraham, God promised, "I will make of thee a great nation, and I will bless thee, and make thy name great" (Genesis 12:2). To have a great name was to be a great nation.

When Moses asked God His name, He answered, "I am that I am" [Jehovah] (Exodus 3:14). That construction appears again in 1 Samuel 23:13, which tells us that David and his men went where they went. It expresses self-determination. In the case of God, His very existence is the product of His will. That phrase, therefore, expresses God's essence. In its absolute self-reference, it also suggests isolation, and it is reassuring that God immediately added that His "name forever" is "the Lord God [Jehovah Elohim] of your fathers, the God of Abraham, the God of Isaac, and the God of Jacob" (Exodus 3:15). He is

---

¹²⁸ Psalm 8:5-6; see also Hebrews 2:7-8.

not only self-existent and eternal, but He eternally relates to us.[129] Isaiah sometimes used the word *name* to mean a sign (Isaiah 55:13) or a reputation (Isaiah 63:12), but when he stated the name of Jesus, he used *name* to describe the essence of Jesus. He said, "His name shall be called Wonderful, Counselor, The Mighty God, The everlasting Father, The Prince of Peace" (Isaiah 9:6). Isaiah used *name* solely to express Jesus' nature and not to state a designation for Jesus since He said that Mary "shall call his name Immanuel" (Isaiah 7:14).[130] Jesus said the Father would send the Holy Spirit "in my name" (John 14:26). He also said, "It is expedient for you that I go away: for if I go not away, the Comforter will not come unto you" (John 16:7), suggesting that the Holy Spirit's coming in Jesus' name is coming in Jesus' place.

God's name stands so much in the place of God as to have the effect of God. David gave the benediction, "The name of the God of Jacob defend thee" (Psalm 20:1). According to Proverbs, "The name of the Lord is a strong tower" (Proverbs 18:10). To think upon the Lord's name is to think upon the Lord. Malachi 3:16. To see God's face in heaven is to have His name on your forehead (Revelation 22:4).

---

[129] God also stated His name, in descriptive terms, to be "Jealous" in Exodus 34:14 and "God Almighty" (El Shaddai) in Exodus 6:3. On Mount Sinai with Moses, God proclaimed His name, as described in Exodus 34:6-7 and noted above.

[130] Jesus gave His name to John, in John's vision on the Isle of Patmos, as "Alpha and Omega, the beginning and the ending . . . which is, and which was, and which is to come, the Almighty" (Revelation 1:8). His name at the battle of Armageddon is "Faithful and True" (Revelation 19:11), "The Word of God" (Revelation 19:13), and "King of Kings and Lord of Lords" (Revelation 19:16).

If *name* merely meant a designation, when Jesus told His brethren to baptize the nations in the name of the Father, the Son, and the Holy Spirit, He meant to immerse converts while saying the names of the members of the Godhead. A closer analysis of baptism, combined with that analysis of the concept of name, shows otherwise.

In contrast to John the Baptist's baptizing with water, John said that Jesus would baptize with the Holy Spirit and fire (Matthew 3:11). "Fire" is a reiteration of the Holy Spirit. At Pentecost, the Holy Spirit came upon the people in "cloven tongues like as of fire" (Acts 2:3). Peter called that event baptism with the Holy Spirit (Acts 11:15-16).

Given that the name of God is in a sense God, and the name of Jesus is in a sense Jesus, and given that the Holy Spirit proceeds from the Father (John 15:26) and is sent in Jesus' place (John 16:7) and therefore is the presence of the Father and the Son among us, to baptize in the name of the Father and the Son and the Holy Spirit is to baptize with the Holy Spirit.

Paul found Ephesians who had been baptized with John's baptism, and he baptized them in the name of Jesus and laid hands on them. The Holy Spirit came upon them, so they spoke in tongues and prophesied (Acts 19:1-6; Acts 8:16-17). Few children of God today have the gift of passing on such spiritual gifts. Nonetheless, we can baptize with the Holy Spirit and pass on the ultimate gift of membership in God's family.

To find out what it means for the children of God to baptize with the Holy Spirit, we return to Matthew 28, which adds, after the reference to baptizing, "teaching them to observe all things whatsoever I have commanded you" (Matthew

28:20). That reaffirms the connection between baptism and the Holy Spirit, whose role is to "teach . . . all things" (John 14:26).

And what are "all things . . . [Jesus] commanded?" Jesus explained the essence: "These things I command you, that ye love one another" (John 15:17; see also John 15:12). He metaphorically said the same thing to Peter when He told Peter three times to feed His sheep. Baptizing in the name of the Father, the Son, and the Holy Spirit is a rich evocation of love on fire. The Great Commission is a commission to love specifically to bring people into God's family, and teach love.

That is not to dismiss immersion, practiced in the early church (see Acts 8:38-39), which serves as a sharing of Jesus' death and resurrection (see Romans 6:4). Instead, it is to understand what happens in baptism beyond the symbolism. When a person rises from baptism to "walk in newness of life" (Romans 6:4), that person experiences the unassailable love of God (Romans 8:39) and love of and for one another (Romans 12:9-21).

Understanding what it means to baptize in the name of the Father and the Son and the Holy Spirit helps us know that what God wants from everyone is love. That love requires a commitment of ourselves from the depths of our selves, not just saying prescribed words.

It also helps us understand that what is provided to the baptized person is a welcome into a loving family. That person has "received the Spirit of adoption, whereby we cry, Abba, Father" (Romans 8:15). As Fanny Crosby expressed it, that person has acquired a blessed assurance that they are "heir of salvation, purchase of God, born of His Spirit, washed in His blood . . . filled with His goodness, lost in His love."

About the Author

Frank Best graduated from Yale College and Penn Law School, and attended the Columbia Business School Executive Program. At his retirement he was General Counsel of Penn Mutual Life Insurance Company. He has written numerous legal articles, and is the author of *Pennsylvania Insurance Law*, published by George T. Bisel Company, and co-author of *Life and Health Insurance Law*, published by Thomson Reuters. This work grew out of a personal Bible study project. Feedback is appreciated, at franklinlbestjr@gmail.com.

Printed in the USA
CPSIA information can be obtained
at www.ICGtesting.com
LVHW050414150224
771724LV00012B/583